People to Know

Andy Warhol

Pioneer of Pop Art

Carin T. Ford

Enslow Publishers, Inc.

40 Industrial Road	PO Box 38
Box 398	Aldershot
Berkeley Heights, NJ 07922	Hants GU12 6BP
USA	UK

http://www.enslow.com

MAR 1 1 2002

J
92W
WARHOL
For

Mt. Lebanon Public Library
Children's Library

Copyright © 2001 by Carin T. Ford

Library of Congress Cataloging-in-Publication Data

Ford, Carin T.
    Andy Warhol : pioneer of pop art / Carin T. Ford.
        p. cm. — (People to know)
    Includes bibliographical references (p.   ) and index.
    ISBN 0-7660-1531-9
    1. Warhol, Andy, 1928–1987—Juvenile literature. 2. Artists—United States—
Biography—Juvenile literature. 3. Pop Art—United States—Juvenile literature.
[1. Warhol, Andy, 1928–1987. 2. Artists. 3. Pop art.] I. Warhol, Andy, 1928–1987.
ill. II. Title. III. Series.
N6537.W28 F67   2001
700'.92—dc21

                                        00-010417

Printed in the United States of America

10 9 8 7 6 5 4 3 2 1

To Our Readers:
All Internet Addresses in this book were active and appropriate when we went to press.
Any comments or suggestions can be sent by e-mail to Comments@enslow.com or to
the address on the back cover.

Illustration Credits: © Corel Corporation, pp. 32, 55; Courtesy of Carnegie
Mellon University Archives, p. 24; Courtesy, Jimmy Carter Library, p. 87;
Library of Congress, p. 15; Photo by Mary Lou Weingarten, pp. 67, 72, 81;
Photofest, pp. 4, 37, 59, 63, 90; Photographed by Michael Schuman in 1994
at the Andy Warhol Museum in Pittsburgh, pp. 9, 17, 46, 51, 75, 83, 92, 96.

Cover Illustration: Christopher Makos

Contents

Andy Warhol, with a self-portrait.

A Can of Soup

It was time to make a change. The year was 1961, and Andy Warhol had been working for more than a decade as an illustrator for newspapers and magazines.

But now he wanted to move beyond the world of advertising. He wanted to be considered a serious artist. And to do that, he needed to come up with an idea—something new, something different.

A movement called Pop Art was taking root in the United States at this time. Artists were trying to bring the real world into their art. They were experimenting with paintings of everyday, commonplace objects. Warhol had tried painting pictures of Coca-Cola bottles and cartoon characters such as Dick Tracy and Popeye. But he was told his pictures were too similar to the work of other artists.

What he needed now was an idea—and he needed one desperately.

Warhol was already a successful commercial artist. He drew illustrations to help sell a variety of products—creating everything from shoe ads and record album covers to greeting cards and book jackets. His apartment overflowed with newspapers, magazines, art supplies, and photographs. It was littered with scores of objects that he had illustrated for advertisements—shoes, gloves, pocketbooks, hats, belts, jewelry, and scarves. Running around in the midst of this clutter were as many as twenty cats, all named Sam. Warhol was earning more money than he was able to keep track of. A friend once rummaged through the disorder and found a check for $700 that Warhol had misplaced and never cashed.[1]

Warhol had been determined to succeed as an artist ever since his arrival in New York in 1949. In the course of twelve years, he had climbed to the top of the commercial art world, earning a considerable amount of money and winning numerous prizes.[2]

But it was not enough.

"I want to be Matisse," he once said, referring to French artist Henri Matisse, who became famous for using color in an unconventional way.

Warhol knew commercial artists could become rich . . . but serious artists could become *famous*. And fame was what he craved.[3]

Feeling desperate and depressed, Warhol asked a friend, interior designer Muriel Latow, for advice. What could he paint that would have a lot of impact and make his work stand out? Latow agreed to help, but she was going to charge a fee for her ideas. When Warhol asked how much it would cost, Latow replied, "Fifty dollars."

"Okay, go ahead," Warhol said, writing out a check for the amount. "Give me a fabulous idea!"[4]

Latow said, "Now, tell me, Andy, what do you love more than anything else?"

Money, he told her.

Latow replied that he should paint money. She also said he should paint something so familiar that people had ceased to notice it. "Something like a can of Campbell's soup," she said.[5]

The idea appealed to Warhol immediately. A painting of a soup can would be basic and straightforward, very different from the elegant illustrations for which he was known.[6] Warhol also enjoyed challenging the traditional ideas of art. If a flower or a bowl of apples could be the subject of a painting, why not a can of Campbell's soup?[7]

He instructed his mother, who shared his apartment, to go to the supermarket and buy every variety of Campbell's soup on the shelves.

Surrounded by each of the thirty-two varieties of soup, Warhol began painting. He experimented with different combinations and sizes of soup cans. Ultimately, he painted a bold portrait of each can of Campbell's soup against a pure white background.

"I wanted to paint nothing," Warhol later said of the soup cans. "I was looking for something that was the essence of nothing, and that was it."[8]

Irving Blum, owner of Ferus Gallery in Los Angeles, California, expressed an interest in showing the soup can pictures at his gallery. Warhol excitedly agreed.

The paintings were put on sale at the gallery for $100 each, one-tenth of the price of Warhol's commercial artwork. Reaction to the soup cans ranged from puzzlement to amusement. A nearby gallery owner purchased several cans of Campbell's soup and put *them* up for sale. He charged sixty cents for three cans. His sign read, "Buy them cheaper here."[9]

Warhol quickly became known throughout the world as the artist who painted the Campbell's soup can. He was even photographed at a supermarket signing his name on an actual can of soup.[10]

Two more shows in New York followed in the fall of 1962, one at the Sidney Janis Gallery and another at the Stable Gallery. By this time, Warhol was becoming known as one of the country's outstanding Pop artists.

Paintings of movie star Marilyn Monroe, dollar bills, Coca-Cola bottles, and soup cans were featured at the shows. Warhol repeated the same image—often one hundred times—on one canvas. His logic seemed to be: If one is good, a hundred must be better.[11]

The Stable Gallery show was Warhol's first one-man exhibition.

"I'll never forget the sight of him coming into the gallery that September, in dirty, filthy clothes and his worn-out sneakers with the laces untied, and a big bunch of canvases rolled up under his arm. . . . Oh,

Warhol's paintings of Campbell's soup cans and Coca-Cola bottles brought him fame as a Pop artist.

he was so *happy* to have a gallery!" said gallery owner Eleanor Ward.[12]

Along with the paintings of soup cans, Coca-Cola bottles, and dollar bills, Warhol's portraits of Marilyn Monroe caught the public's attention. The famous movie star had died that summer, and Warhol made numerous portraits of her. In one work, he covered a twelve-foot canvas with one hundred images of Monroe's face. He used extremely bright colors for her lips, hair, and eyes. In another, he used the repeated image of her lips alone.

"I like boring things," Warhol once said. "I like things to be exactly the same over and over again."[13]

Public reaction to this show was markedly different

from the one in Los Angeles. People were not simply confused and curious. Now many people claimed they loved his pictures; many others hated them.

"Isn't it the most ghastly thing you've ever seen in your life?" a Museum of Modern Art employee asked his colleague, referring to a Monroe portrait.

"Yes, isn't it?" the colleague agreed. "I bought one."[14]

Perhaps because of the controversy, nearly all the pictures in the show were sold.

With these gallery openings, Warhol was on his way to becoming one of the most famous and influential artists in the world. His career would span virtually every medium—painting, sculpting, writing, magazine publishing, moviemaking, and photography.

Yet years later, Warhol said that he only hoped to be remembered as a can of soup.[15]

Pittsburgh

In the early 1900s, the people of Pittsburgh, Pennsylvania, had come to expect the sky to be pitch black. The big, rough city was the steel and coal capital of the United States. Rarely was the sun able to penetrate the thick blanket of smog that filled the sky.[1] The streets were grimy and crowded with trolleys and horse-drawn carriages.

The steel industry dominated Pittsburgh, and many immigrants, searching for work and a better way of life, flocked to the city. It became a classic melting pot, with its number of foreign-born citizens doubling between 1880 and 1900. Years earlier, immigrants from Ireland, Scandinavia, and Germany had settled there. But by the turn of the century, immigrants from Poland, Hungary, Slovakia, Italy, and other European countries were arriving in droves.

Life for these immigrants was not easy. In fact, it would have been difficult for the situation to be worse. Arriving with little money and frequently unable to speak English, the immigrants were forced to live in crowded tenement houses. It was not unusual for twelve or more people to share a single room.[2]

The city did not have adequate sanitation facilities, so diseases—including deadly typhoid fever—spread easily. There were not enough schools for the children; there was not enough fire or police protection. Fighting occurred on a daily basis between longtime Pittsburgh residents and the immigrants who had come in hopes of making better lives for themselves.

Andrei Warhola was one of these immigrants.

He had traveled to Pittsburgh in 1906 at the age of seventeen, leaving behind his small village of Medzilaborce in what is now Slovakia. The Ruthenians lived off the land, raising livestock and growing crops. Their houses were made of wood and had straw roofs. Each house was surrounded by a fence that was adorned with repeated images of stars, flowers, and crosses.[3]

In Pittsburgh, Andrei Warhola became a coal miner and worked in the mines for two years. He then traveled back across the ocean and returned to his village, marrying sixteen-year-old Julia Zavacky in 1909. Like her husband, Julia Zavacky came from a family of farmers and goatherds. She had spent much time as a child helping her fourteen brothers and sisters guard the goats from wolves.[4] They lived in Czechoslovakia for three years until Andrei Warhola headed back to Pittsburgh, leaving his wife behind. He planned to send for her as soon as he had earned enough money to pay for her passage.

These years were hard for Julia Warhola. Her first child died in infancy, and because of poor crops, she was forced to live on potatoes and bread. When World War I erupted in 1914, Julia often had to flee into the nearby forests for several days in order to hide from enemy soldiers. By 1921, Julia had managed to borrow enough money to make the journey to the United States. Unable to speak English, she traveled by horse cart, train, and ship until she arrived in Pittsburgh.[5]

Julia and Andrei Warhola already had two sons—Paul, born in 1922, and John, born in 1925—when Andy was born. Like many facts concerning Andy's life, information about his birth is contradictory.

Andy would always enjoy the mystery and confusion surrounding his life. "I never give my background, and anyway, I make it all up different every time I'm asked," he said.[6] At various times, he told reporters that his birthplace was Cleveland, Philadelphia, Pittsburgh, and even Hawaii. But his baptism certificate shows that he was born on August 6, 1928, in the Pittsburgh neighborhood of Soho.

Like most immigrants in the early 1900s, the Warholas worked hard for their money. Andrei Warhola's wages were low and the family struggled to make ends meet. Their home consisted of two rooms and was covered with tarpaper; there was no indoor bathroom. Julia Warhola cleaned houses for $2 a day and also earned money by making flowers out of tin cans and selling them for a quarter. In the backyard, she grew cabbages, beets, and carrots. Andrei Warhola repaired the children's shoes with rubber he obtained from used tires. Paul and John took jobs selling newspapers, delivering ice, and carrying coal.

Andrei Warhola's job for the construction and house-moving firm of John Eichleay Company often required him to be gone from the family for weeks at a time. Traveling throughout the midwestern and New England states, he was once absent from home for six months.[7] Paul, the oldest son, took charge of the family during their father's absence. He decided to send four-year-old Andy to school—even though most children did not begin until the age of six.

It took one day at Soho Elementary School to convince Andy he did not like it. After a girl hit him, he refused to go back. Considered a crybaby throughout his childhood, Andy sobbed to his mother that he wanted to stay with her. Julia Warhola decided to keep her son home for the next two years. She enjoyed drawing, and the two spent much of their time together drawing pictures. A neighbor who used to baby-sit for Andy remarked, "He was really a handful to watch, a sprightly, rambunctious, high-strung type."[8]

By the time Andy turned six, the family had moved to a nicer neighborhood and a larger house. He entered Holmes Elementary School and started in the second grade. His one day at the old elementary

Andy Warhol grew up in Pittsburgh, Pennsylvania. His family was very poor when he was born.

school had mistakenly been considered a full year. Extremely pale with fair hair, Andy was very shy but appeared to be well liked.

"He was very quiet, not at all outgoing, and he was real good in drawing," said Catherine Metz, one of Andy's teachers.[9] After school, he would do his homework and then spend the rest of his time drawing pictures.

At the age of seven, Andy asked his mother to buy him a cartoon projector. Julia saved money from her work cleaning houses until she had the $20 she needed for the projector. The family could not afford a screen, so Andy showed Mickey Mouse and Little Orphan Annie cartoons on the wall. Often, these cartoons would give him ideas for his sketches.

Andy became ill the following year with chorea, a nervous disorder that causes uncontrollable movements of the arms, legs, and face. The illness developed as a result of rheumatic fever, and Andy began to experience shaking limbs, slurred speech, and buckling at the knees. He had difficulty coordinating such movements as writing or tying his shoes, and he was kept home from school for a month in order to rest.

"We were real worried about him, but what do you do . . . ," recalled Paul Warhola. "They just says, 'Leave him rest around in bed.' That's when we bought him books to cut out and color and magazine books, in order to keep him comfortable and occupied."[10]

Andy enjoyed his time at home. He said later that he would lie in bed with a favorite doll while his mother "would read to me in her thick Czechoslovakian accent as best she could and I would always say, 'Thanks, Mom,' after she finished with Dick Tracy, even if I hadn't understood a word."[11]

Andy never seemed to grow tired of the coloring books, paper dolls, and movie magazines Julia Warhola bought for him. Every time Andy finished a page in his coloring book, Julia would reward him with a chocolate candy bar.

As for the paper dolls, Andy said, "I never used to cut out my cut-out dolls . . . I didn't want to ruin the nice pages they were on. I always left my cut-out dolls in my cut-out books."[12]

As a sickly little boy, Andy spent many days at home doing artwork with his mother. Many years later, when Warhol made silk-screens of famous people, he included his mother, Julia Warhola (middle), in the collection.

Paul Warhola said he showed Andy how to put wax directly onto a comic strip and then rub it. The image on the wax could then be transferred to another piece of paper. "Yeah, I'd sit with him and play with him," he said. "We didn't have a radio then or nothing."[13]

Andy's physical condition gradually improved. Soon, he was able to hold scissors and would spend hours making collages with cutout magazine pictures. He also copied comic strips by covering them with wax and then rubbing and tracing the image onto a clean sheet of paper. Years later, Andy would become known for creating paintings out of transferred images.

He was sent back to school after a month. But soon, when the shaking in his limbs resumed, it became apparent that he needed more time to recuperate. Although Andy enjoyed being back home for another month, he continued to be weak. He developed large reddish patches all over his body. This skin condition would stay with him throughout his life.

But other children liked Andy because of his ability to draw. He frequently had his neighbors and cousins sit for him so he could do their portraits.

Once Andy was well, he seemed to spend as much time as possible at the movies. To earn the eleven cents he needed for a ticket, Andy would help his brothers sell peanuts for a penny a bag at baseball games. One of his favorite movie stars was Shirley Temple, a child actress who was famous for her singing and dancing. Andy became a member of her fan club.

When Andy was thirteen, his father came down with hepatitis, a disease that can damage the liver. After being ill for several months, Andrei Warhola died. Following tradition, his body was brought into the house for a three-day viewing. Andy remained hidden under his bed during this time.

John later recalled a conversation with his father a few days before his death: Andrei Warhola insisted "that Andy's gonna be highly educated" and that "there's enough money to start him off in school."[14]

Andy's natural interest in art was encouraged by various programs offered in Pittsburgh. The Carnegie Museum of Art held Saturday morning art classes at no cost, and Andy began attending on the recommendation of his elementary school art teacher. The weekend classes were taught by Joseph Fitzpatrick, who instructed his students in the basic concepts of drawing and painting.

"A more talented person than Andy Warhol I never knew," said Fitzpatrick. "I encouraged him to do whatever he wanted to do because he was so individualistic."[15]

These classes provided the spark that Andy needed. By the time he entered Schenley High School in 1941, he was drawing constantly. All his spare time was spent on his art, and he often ignored his mother's calls to come down to dinner. So Julia would bring Andy's meals up to his room. His room was filled with his drawings, and he carried a sketchbook wherever he went.

Although he was small and frail looking, Andy was able to protect himself from some of the tougher boys in the neighborhood with his artwork. Rather than pick on Andy, they frequently gathered around, watching admiringly as he sketched.

"When I think of my high school days," he said, "all I can remember really, are the long walks to school, through the Czechoslovakian ghetto with the babushkas and overalls on the clotheslines. . . . I wasn't amazingly popular, but I had some nice friends."[16]

When he was in his final year of high school, Andy was accepted for admission to both the Carnegie Institute of Technology and the University of Pittsburgh. He chose Carnegie Tech because it had the better art department. Julia paid the tuition with a $15,000 postal bond left by her husband specifically for Andy's education. Andy also earned some money by working at a small restaurant making sandwiches and milk shakes.

Although Andy was eager to attend Carnegie Tech, he immediately began having difficulty with his academic subjects. He also found himself in trouble with his art teachers.

College

"**I**f anyone had asked me at the time who was the least likely to succeed, I would have said Andy Warhola," commented Robert Lepper, an art teacher at Carnegie Tech.[1]

Faculty members of the art department could not make up their minds about Andy. Did his work show talent and unique creativity? Or were his projects the careless efforts of a young man who was completely unable to draw?

"In a classroom of thirty, it was easy to overlook Andy; though tall enough to be counted, he was so quiet that he often seemed to be virtually nonverbal," said Bennard B. Perlman, who attended Carnegie Tech at the same time as Andy. "I came to think of him as one who let his art do the talking."[2]

Sometimes Andy would hand in a project that had nothing to do with the assignment. Other times, he would turn in work that contained ripped pieces of construction paper attached by tape, or papers covered with paw prints made by his own cat.

Some members of the art department wanted Andy dropped from the college. They felt the work he was producing was not acceptable. Others disagreed, and whenever a vote was taken, the motion to dismiss him always failed. Andy remained in school.

His difficulties continued, however, with his academic subjects. During his first year at Carnegie Tech, Andy's courses were Drawing I, Pictorial and Decorative Design, Color, Hygiene, and Thought and Expression.

Andy had the disadvantage of coming from a home where his mother barely spoke English. He could not speak correctly, much less write well. He enlisted the aid of two friends—Gretchen Schmertz and Ellie Simon—to help him with his papers for his Thought and Expression class. The ideas were Andy's, but the writing was done by the young women.[3]

Andy spent that first year of college in much the same way he had spent high school. He rarely spoke, and adolescence had not improved his looks. The shapeless blue jeans, ragged work shirt, and old sneakers he wore every day did not help either. A case of acne contributed to earning him the nickname "Andy the red nosed Warhola."[4]

He continued to spend most of his free time on his art, and this generally occurred at night. Andy enjoyed working at night for two important reasons. First, there were fewer interruptions; second, he was afraid of the dark. Throughout Andy's life, he would spend most of the nighttime hours awake.

At the end of Andy's freshman year, soldiers who had fought in World War II were now returning home to the United States. They were eager to enter college on the GI Bill. When the soldiers arrived, some students had to be dropped. Because the art department could handle only one hundred students, two-thirds of Andy's class was asked to leave. Andy, who had poor grades in all his subjects, was one of them.

He was devastated at the news but soon had reason to be optimistic. As a result of several teachers' recommendations, Andy was told he could go to summer school and repeat the Thought and Expression class he had failed. He would also be expected to work on his art and hand in several projects by the end of summer. If the quality of his work were acceptable, he would be allowed to enroll again in the fall.

That summer, Andy divided his time between working and drawing. Occasionally the two were combined. He had a job selling fruits and vegetables for his brother Paul. Earning $3 a day, Andy would help Paul load the truck in the morning and then drive around selling the produce door-to-door. While Andy worked, he carried a sketchbook. He would use a "speed-sketching" method of drawing that he had been taught at school. Never lifting his pencil from the paper, he could sketch people in just ten seconds. His drawings focused on the people he saw—women in ragged clothing, and babies clinging to their mothers.

When Andy submitted this notebook of sketches to the art department in the fall, he was allowed to return to Carnegie Tech. In addition, the drawings were put on display at the school and Andy received a prize of $40. An article in the *Pittsburgh Press* read "Artist-Huckster sketches customers and wins prize."[5] This would be the first of Andy's many experiences with publicity.

These events brought attention to Andy, and he became part of a circle of art students. Gretchen Schmertz, who had helped write Andy's papers and was a member of the circle, described Andy as "this

Andy studied art at Carnegie Institute of Technology, where one of his friends said he "drew like an angel."

kid who just drew like an angel. He had his own quality of line, this wonderful shaggy, jagged line."[6]

He often worked at the home of his friend Philip Pearlstein, who would later become a well-known realist painter. "He didn't have room at home," Pearlstein said. "There were some nieces and nephews who wouldn't let him work in peace, and they'd destroy his work. His brothers made fun of him—they thought he was strange because he was doing art."[7]

Gaining confidence, Andy began taking an interest in cultural events. He became a member of a film club at the college and watched movies from New York's Museum of Modern Art. He went to performances of Pittsburgh's symphony orchestra and attended ballet and modern dance recitals. He was the only young man to be a member of the Modern Dance Club, and he also became art director of the school's literary magazine, *Cano*.

That summer, he moved into a studio with four other art students. The rental fee was $10 for two and a half months. Each student had his own separate area for working. Andy devoted himself to art that summer of 1947 and produced numerous paintings of children.

Also at this time, he developed a blotted-line technique of drawing, which would eventually be the basis of his commercial art. The technique involved drawing a picture in ink on one piece of paper, pressing this paper face down onto a clean sheet of paper, and rubbing hard to duplicate the image.

The reproduced drawing had a smudged, slightly broken-up look to it because not all the ink was transferred evenly. What pleased Andy most about this technique was that he had not really drawn the final picture. He liked knowing that he had produced a work of art without actually touching his pen to the final paper. This separation of the artist from his art would be a recurring theme throughout Andy's career. It would become more noticeable as the years went on.

Another indication of Andy's later style was seen in his handling of one of his assignments. Pictorial design professor Robert Lepper told his students to choose any house on any street and envision the family that lived there. Then, they were to draw the living room. Andy simply walked to his own street, selected his own house, and made a drawing in pastels of his family's living room.[8]

Andy was hired the following spring to paint the background scenery for the display windows of Joseph Horne, a large Pittsburgh department store. Larry Vollmer, the store's display director, recognized Andy's talent, though he felt sorry for the young man's unattractive appearance. Vollmer told Andy to browse through copies of *Vogue* and *Harper's Bazaar* magazines, looking for ideas. The magazines expanded Andy's sense of style.

Andy enjoyed the job and the work suited him, in spite of the fact that he was not a fast worker. This job at the department store gave him excellent training for the years he would soon be spending as a commercial artist. It also taught him that working quickly was a priority in the field.

Finishing his final year at Carnegie Tech, Andy continued working on his drawings and paintings. Many were considered unsuitable for display, but Andy persisted in producing art that *he* wanted to create. He developed a reputation for painting pictures that were scandalous. His fame grew when he submitted a picture for the annual Pittsburgh Associated Artists' exhibition. The painting of a boy with his finger in his nose was titled *The Broad Gave Me My Face, But I Can Pick My Own Nose.* In a pattern that was becoming familiar, half the artists who were judging the exhibition rejected the work as inappropriate, while the other half considered it a painting that should be taken seriously.

Although two of Andy's paintings had been included in the exhibition the year before, *The Broad Gave Me My Face . . .* was not. Andy's failure to qualify for the show, however, only increased his popularity as an artist.

A few months later, Andy exhibited the painting, retitled *Why Pick on Me?*, in a local group show. People "just *flocked* to see this painting . . . it was so controversial," said Robert Fleischer, also a student at Carnegie Tech.[9]

Andy's four years at Carnegie Tech were nearly over, and he had to decide what to do with his life. His real interest lay in finding work in New York City, but he doubted he was good enough. Andy considered getting a job as an art teacher, and he applied to an art school in Indiana. But the school sent back the portfolio of Andy's drawings and paintings and turned down his application.

Andy then decided to take a chance.

He was going to New York.

New York

Andy Warhola—who would soon call himself Andy Warhol—had been in New York City for only two days when he met with Tina Fredericks, an art director at *Glamour* magazine.

Fredericks later said that she suspected Warhol approached the magazine because it was known for its features of Hollywood movie stars at that time. "Even as a sickly child, Andy worshipped the idols of the silver—his favorite color—screen," Fredericks said. "So probably it was no more than the name "Glamour" that made him call . . . for glamour was surely what he loved."[1]

She recalled greeting "a pale, blotchy boy, diffident almost to the point of disappearance but somehow immediately and immensely appealing. He seemed all one color: pale chinos, pale wispy hair, pale eyes."[2] He carried a big, black portfolio containing his blotted-line drawings of people and flowers. "His ink lines were electrifying," said Fredericks. "Fragmented, broken, and intriguing, they grabbed at you with their spontaneous intensity."[3]

Although Fredericks was fascinated by Warhol's portfolio and aware of his talent, she was looking for artwork of everyday objects. She asked Warhol if he could draw something more practical.

"I can draw *anything*," he answered.[4]

He was given an assignment to draw shoes and took home six shoes to use as models. It was important that Warhol do a good job. He had managed to save $200, which would pay for his expenses through the summer. This included the apartment he had rented with fellow Carnegie Tech graduate Philip Pearlstein. Once the $200 ran out, Warhol would need to rely on his talent as an artist to support himself.

He returned to Fredericks the following day with a collection of shoe drawings stuffed into a brown paper bag. According to the art director, the pictures were beautiful and ornate.[5] But they were not what Fredericks had in mind. She wanted shoes that were sleek, modern, and sophisticated. Warhol hurried back to his apartment and returned the next day with shoes drawn exactly as Fredericks had requested. She hired him to do six more pages.

"He was *fast*, and that, in combination with intelligent, adaptable, and really good, made him an art director's dream come true," she said.[6]

Warhol went on countless interviews, wearing a pair of wrinkled chino pants, a baggy T-shirt, and old sneakers. He carried a portfolio of artwork in a brown paper bag. Showing up for an interview at *Harper's Bazaar*, he opened the paper bag to display his work and a cockroach crawled out. Andy claimed the editor felt sorry for him and gave him the job.[7]

It did not take long for Warhol's name to become known throughout New York City. Jobs for other magazines quickly followed.

He was given assignments for *Seventeen* and *Charm* magazines, along with several record album covers for Columbia Records. He threw himself into every project, creating not just one drawing but several alternatives, and he would present all of them to the art directors.

According to singer Lou Reed, who would later work with the artist, Warhol always seemed to possess endless energy. "He had a very intense work ethic that he was always drumming into us," Reed said. "If I wrote a song, he'd say, 'Why didn't you write five songs?' He said, 'Work is everything. Work is the entire thing.'"[8]

Although his roommate, Pearlstein, advised Warhol to enhance his appearance and buy a suit, Warhol stuck to the chinos, T-shirts, and sneakers he had worn to his *Glamour* interview. He continued carrying his assignments in a brown paper bag. This led to his friends' nicknaming him "Raggedy Andy" and "Andy Paperbag."[9]

By the summer of 1949, Warhol was spending every day actively searching for new assignments.

"I can draw anything," said Warhol, who began his career as a commercial artist in New York City.

Pearlstein was working full-time for a graphic designer. Several other friends from Carnegie Tech had also moved to New York. They were working as children's book illustrators or jewelry designers. Occasionally, they questioned whether the work Warhol was doing was "real art." But to Warhol, his commercial work was no different from fine art.

Pearlstein got married the following year and Warhol moved into a crowded apartment of dancers. Despite the constant confusion of the living arrangements, Warhol worked at an orderly drafting table with carefully arranged pens and brushes.

"All I remember is Andy sitting there drawing, surrounded by this complete chaos and people doing things that would seem to be disruptive of any concentration. The food was mixed in with the clothes," recalled a friend.[10]

Warhol enjoyed the chaos, although he remained very shy and rarely spoke to his roommates. One girl living in the apartment said she became so irritated with Warhol for not speaking to her that she hit him in the head with an egg.[11]

He continued his college habit of working through the night and sleeping during the day. But the long hours he spent at his drafting table took their toll on his eyes. Following the advice of *Glamour* art director Tina Fredericks, Warhol made an appointment with an eye doctor and began wearing glasses with thick lenses.

A year later, Warhol moved again when his apartment building was about to be demolished. He roomed with Joseph Groell, a painter who had graduated from Carnegie Tech. This would be another in a long line of moves for Warhol during the next few years.

Throughout the early 1950s, Warhol continued working on a variety of assignments that earned him a considerable amount of money and ever-increasing recognition. Plus, he enjoyed the work.

"I loved working when I worked at commercial art," said Warhol, "and they told you what to do and how to do it and all you had to do was correct it and they'd say yes or no. . . . That makes everything easy when you're working."[12]

He designed several book jackets and was asked to illustrate the *Complete Book of Etiquette* by Amy Vanderbilt. He won the Art Directors' Club gold medal for his drawing of a sailor addicted to drugs. *The New York Times* ran a full-page spread of the picture, which was being used to advertise a radio show about crime. When a recording was made of the program, Warhol's drawing was used on the album cover.

In 1952, Julia Warhola moved in with her son, who by now had an apartment of his own. Julia Warhola took over the cooking and housework, while Warhol concentrated completely on his art. He had done numerous illustrations based on author Truman Capote's books, and he decided to show them to Alexandre Iolas, an art dealer. The result was Warhol's first gallery opening on June 16, 1952. The show was called "15 Drawings Based on the Writings of Truman Capote." Warhol invited Capote, whom he admired, to attend. But the author did not come.

If Warhol's friends were still questioning the validity of his work, the gallery show helped prove he was serious about producing fine art—in spite of the fact that none of the pictures sold. Calling Warhol's work "fragile impressions," James Fitzsimmons of *Art Digest* wrote: "At its best it is an art that depends upon . . . the communication of intangibles and ambivalent feelings."[13]

Warhol hired an agent, Fritzie Miller, the following year. Miller landed her client assignments with *McCall's, Ladies' Home Journal, Vogue,* and *Harper's Bazaar.* Warhol soon became "the most sought-after illustrator of women's accessories in New York," according to Calvin Tomkins of *The New Yorker* magazine.[14]

At twenty-five, Warhol now earned a yearly income of more than $25,000. He was unused to having a surplus of money, and he spent it inconsistently. Warhol would treat himself to extravagant meals at some of New York's fancier restaurants, as well as expensive front-row seats to Broadway shows. But he continued wearing the same tattered clothing and living in a poorly furnished apartment. To celebrate Thanksgiving with his mother, Warhol took her to the lunch counter at Woolworth's five-and-dime store.

Warhol eventually moved to a larger apartment, although he and his mother continued their habit of sleeping on mattresses placed on the floor. The rooms quickly became cluttered with art supplies, magazines, and all the accessories Warhol used for his illustrations. Money was left lying around and numerous cats had the run of the apartment. The phonograph and television were usually on, and visitors were instantly assaulted by the smell, the noise, and the lack of a place to sit down.[15]

Warhol's days were full. Most mornings, he would attend an early church service, eat a breakfast made by his mother, and put in a few hours of work. He would then dress in a ragged T-shirt and chinos and head out to an ad agency or visit an art director at a magazine. Occasionally, he had business lunches followed by a visit to another office to get the necessary materials for an assignment. At night, Warhol went to the theater or the ballet or to a party. Then, he would go home and work until close to dawn.

He had three more shows in 1954 at the Loft Gallery, consisting of drawings and marbled-paper sculptures. Members of the fine art community paid little attention to the shows. But commercial art directors of major agencies were extremely interested. When they tried to speak to Warhol, however, they found conversation was difficult for the shy artist. Tina Fredericks recalled that in all the years she knew Warhol, she never had a "real" conversation with him. He spoke almost exclusively in short exclamations such as "Gee," "Wow," "Really?" "Oh," "Ah," and "Er."[16]

It was around this time that Warhol began wearing wigs to hide his baldness. He would eventually own several hundred wigs in all colors. One of the most commonly recognized ones was a long, unruly silver gray hairpiece that was usually worn slightly off to one side. Warhol would always be self-conscious about his looks. He began working out at a local YMCA three times a week.

Warhol's name became even more prominent when he began drawing weekly advertisements for I. Miller, a shoe store located on Fifth Avenue. The ads appeared in the society pages of the Sunday *New York Times* and Warhol was paid $50,000 a year for them, which was a tremendous amount of money at the time. He used his first paycheck to buy one hundred white shirts—all identical—from Brooks Brothers.[17]

Warhol was able to find a use for the drawings that were not wanted by I. Miller. He sold them in a coffee shop for up to $25 each. According to George Hartman, who worked in advertising, the I. Miller ads

Warhol was a shy man, and he was self-conscious about his appearance. He spoke in short phrases like "Gee," "Wow," "Really?" "Oh," and "Er."

made Warhol "the most successful, imitated, and adulated illustrator" of commercial art in New York.[18]

Warhol's work was varied. He designed stationery for Bergdorf Goodman, a department store, and created Christmas cards for Tiffany's and Tiber Press. He even appeared on television, or, at least, his hand did. Warhol drew suns and clouds on the weather chart for an early morning news program. He needed to wake up at five o'clock because his hand required makeup—its color was too white.[19]

In 1955, he illustrated a book called *A la Recherche du Shoe Perdu* (which means, in French, Searching for the Lost Shoe). Shoes were a common theme in Warhol's early work. He created a series of drawings called "Crazy Golden Slippers," where different shoes were associated with different celebrities. For example, singer Elvis Presley inspired a pirate-style boot, while a fancy high-heeled shoe represented actress and singer Julie Andrews. Warhol trimmed the shoes with leaves of gold and silver and made them extremely fashionable and refined.[20]

The following year, Warhol had a show of these shoes at the Bodley Gallery. The drawings were priced between $50 and $225. The artist was surprised and pleased that many of them were bought for decorations.

But success in the commercial art world only encouraged Warhol to aspire to something more. He wanted to be accepted as a true artist. The only question was: How?

5

The Prince of Pop

Only a few years earlier, Warhol had been enjoying his greatest success as an artist. But the end of the decade saw a decided turn in his career.

He opened a show called "Wild Raspberries" in December 1959 at David Mann's gallery. Labeled "clever frivolity" by *The New York Times*, the show was composed of pictures of various types of foods. Handwritten "recipes" by Julia Warhola appeared beneath each drawing. Warhol published a book by himself of the pictures, but he was unable to find anyone interested in buying copies of it.[1] Instead, he gave the books to friends and colleagues as gifts.

Then a new art director took over at I. Miller shoes and decided to change the company's image. He did not want Warhol to draw the advertisements anymore; he wanted to hire a new illustrator. Since Warhol had recently bought an expensive townhouse on Lexington Avenue, money was tight. He needed to find as many commercial art assignments as possible. Another concern was that his mother, who continued living with him, had begun drinking heavily. Because of Warhol's busy schedule, Julia Warhola had little company except for the television. She lived an isolated and lonely life.[2]

Warhol was worried that he would never receive the recognition as a painter that he had always wanted. He knew he needed to create something that would stand out. He believed that his success as a commercial artist and his open homosexuality excluded him from the art scene. In the 1950s, the public declaration that a man was gay could easily destroy his career.

"I've got to think of something different," Warhol told a friend.[3]

The timing was perfect for Pop Art.

Pop Art was an artistic movement that had begun a decade earlier in England. Lawrence Alloway, an English art critic, was the first to call certain works "Pop Art." "Pop" meant "popular" and included objects found in everyday life, as well as products of the mass media.[4] The name stuck, and in spite of the negative reactions of most art critics, so did the movement.

In 1957, British artist Richard Hamilton listed the characteristics of Pop Art:

Popular (designed for a mass audience)
Transient (short-term solution)

Expendable (easily forgotten)
Low-Cost
Mass-Produced
Young (aimed at youth)
Witty
Sexy
Gimmicky
Glamorous
Big Business[5]

In the United States, specifically New York City, Pop Art reached its full potential during the 1960s.[6] Artists such as Robert Rauschenberg, Jasper Johns, Roy Lichtenstein, and Claes Oldenburg started producing "everyday" art by painting comic strips, street signs, lightbulbs, and items that could be found in any supermarket aisle.

Where did this idea come from?

Before Pop Art, the main artistic movement of the time was Abstract Expressionism. The artists who created Abstract Expressionism had little interest in painting common objects like cereal boxes. Instead, they experimented with color, design, rhythm, and innovative methods of applying paint.

Artists such as Jackson Pollock did not even use brushes when creating paintings. Using regular house paint, Pollock would pour or fling the paint onto an enormous canvas that he had spread on his floor. There was no real composition to these paintings; they consisted of a network of colors.[7]

"The painting has a life of its own," Pollock said, explaining his technique. "I try to let it come through."[8]

Willem de Kooning was another well-known Abstract Expressionist and a friend of Pollock's. He created paintings that also had a spontaneous look and were created with equally obvious freedom.[9] These bold techniques reflected a strong belief in freedom of expression.

The paintings were generally well received by art critics and other artists. But it was not the kind of art the public could easily understand.[10]

The Pop artists—most of whom were trained in commercial art—were not interested in abstract ideas that opened people's minds. They wanted to bring the real world back into art.[11] These artists looked at the society around them and saw a culture that was obsessed with youth. It was dependent upon the mass manufacture of cheap, throw-away products.

Inflatable chairs, paper dresses, and soda cans were symbols of the times. No home was complete without a television; synthetic materials such as nylon and plastic-laminated surfaces made life simpler and easier. Convenience foods like Jell-O were popular in most homes. Life had become quick, easy, and disposable.[12] The artists observed this and then they painted it.

Pop Art dominated American culture from 1962 through 1966. Because it was so accessible and easy to understand, Pop Art established itself more quickly than any other movement in art history.[13]

Conditions could not have been better for Warhol. Here was his chance to make fine art out of commercial art. Interestingly, he had already begun working in the Pop style, unaware that other artists were doing the same thing.

At the start of the 1960s, Warhol visited Leo Castelli's gallery to buy a painting by another Pop artist, Jasper Johns. Warhol noticed two paintings of comic strips that had been done by Roy Lichtenstein. He commented in a shocked voice to Ivan Karp, the gallery's associate director, "Ohhh, I'm doing work just like that myself."[14]

Warhol had painted a series of pictures based on cartoons he had enjoyed as a child: *Little Nancy, Popeye,* and *Dick Tracy.* The paintings were large, and he used drips and splashes to cover up the words.

He had also made paintings based on magazine advertisements of canned foods, televisions, wigs, and nose jobs. He first made a slide of the image, then projected the image onto white canvas. Next, he took black paint and traced over the image, ignoring any drips or splatters.

When Emile de Antonio, an agent for artists, saw one of Warhol's six-foot canvases of a black and white Coca-Cola bottle, he described it as "remarkable. . . . It's our society, it's who we are. It's absolutely beautiful and naked."[15]

Not everyone agreed with de Antonio's assessment of Warhol's work. The agent's wife felt her husband was wasting his time on Warhol. But de Antonio said later, "Andy was blindingly ambitious. I was sure he was going to make it, although not necessarily in art—he could have made it in just about anything he tried."[16]

De Antonio took other important members of the

art world to Warhol's home to see his paintings. Ivan Karp and Henry Geldzahler, an assistant curator at the Metropolitan Museum of Art, were impressed with what they saw. But they were slightly taken aback by the environment in which the artist worked, with the television, radio, and phonograph all blaring. Warhol also enjoyed welcoming guests while wearing an eighteenth-century mask of feathers and jewels. He encouraged visitors to wear masks as well.

Warhol sold several pictures, and through Geldzahler he had them shown to various art galleries. Still, he was not gaining the foothold in the world of Pop Art that he had hoped for. Warhol's reputation as a commercial artist was deeply ingrained in the art community. Some gallery owners were concerned that their own reputations would be harmed by showing the work of a less-than-serious artist.

Karp finally persuaded gallery owner Leo Castelli to look at Warhol's paintings. Arriving at the townhouse, Castelli was greeted by Warhol, who was wearing the eighteenth-century mask. Castelli was interested in Warhol's work but felt it was too similar to Lichtenstein's paintings. These were also based on advertisements and comic strips. Castelli refused to show Warhol's pictures in his gallery.

"You will take me. I'll be back," Warhol told Castelli.[17]

That is when the artist turned to Muriel Latow, an interior designer who ran her own gallery. Latow suggested painting pictures of money and soup cans, and Warhol responded enthusiastically.

He made no attempt to hide the fact that he merely

acted as the middleman in his paintings. Warhol's goal was always to detach himself—his thoughts, emotions, and actual hand—as much as possible from his work.

He was also trying to detach the spectator from the painting. By repeating images over and over on the canvas, Warhol removed all the emotion. Even his later works of car accidents and electric chairs leave the viewer feeling numb and uninvolved, rather than horrified.[18]

"Machines have less problems. I'd like to be a machine, wouldn't you?" Warhol said.[19]

For this reason, Warhol began silk-screening his pictures. "I wanted something stronger that gave more of an assembly-line effect," he said.[20]

Silk-screening was similar to his earlier method of making slides of images and then projecting them onto a canvas. But using slides took time. With silk-screening, Warhol was able to achieve the same result in only a few minutes.

Warhol began the process by placing a mesh screen directly onto a blank canvas. The screen contained a photographic image. Paint was applied over the screen with a rubber squeegee. The paint was then forced through the screen onto the canvas beneath. Silk screens of the same image had many variations depending on how worn the squeegee had become, how much pressure was exerted on the squeegee, and at what angle it had been held. Warhol often deliberately sought out these variations.[21]

Occasionally, he reversed the process. He would first apply paint directly to the canvas for the background

Warhol used shocking colors and often created grotesque images. He repeated pictures over and over to dull their emotional impact.

and then put the silk-screened image on top of this. Not only did the method suit Warhol, but it seemed a reflection of sixties culture: fast and easy, cheap and mass-produced.[22]

"The artificial fascinates me, the bright and shiny," Warhol said.[23]

Pop Art had arrived with a bang in America. Not only was Warhol part of the explosion, but he had rapidly become the most famous Pop artist of all.[24]

Yet his explanations of himself and his work would always remain elusive. An interviewer asked him, "Do you think Pop Art is—"

"No," said Warhol.

"What?"

"No."

The interviewer began again, "Do you think Pop Art is—"

"No," said Warhol. "No, I don't."[25]

In spite of his ever-increasing fame, some members of the art world—including several of Warhol's friends—still questioned the importance of his work.

"I told him, 'I think it's wonderful what you're doing,'" said a friend, "'Just tell me in your heart of hearts you know it isn't art.'"[26]

Warhol's answer was simply to paint. And he continued to remain mechanical and uninvolved. "When I have to think about it, I know the picture is wrong. . . . Some people, they paint abstract, so they sit there thinking about it because thinking makes them feel they're doing something. But my thinking never makes me feel I'm doing anything," he said.[27]

Further stressing the separation of the artist from the art, Warhol painted a series called *Do It Yourself.* The paintings were based on paint-by-number diagrams; the numbers indicated the different colors used in each area.

During the summer of 1963, he painted a series of portraits of Elvis Presley. There were six-foot pictures of Elvis in silver holding a gun, and there were pictures of soup cans with Elvis's face on the label.

He also began painting pictures of disasters, such as *129 Die in Jet*, which was based on a *New York Daily News* headline. Other paintings included car crashes, funerals, and the hydrogen bomb. He used bold, shocking colors, creating grotesque images with such titles as *Vertical Orange Car Crash, Purple Jumping Man, Green Disaster Twice.* Frequently, the same image was repeated over and over.

Although some of his work was pornographic or in very poor taste, Warhol continually denied there was any meaning behind his choice of subjects. Instead, he appeared to be trying to erase all meaning.

"The more you look at the same thing, the more the meaning goes away, and the better and emptier you feel," he said.[28]

Warhol had a gallery show in Paris, France, in 1964. He was now becoming internationally famous.

"Warhol captured the imagination of the media and the public as had no other artist of his generation," said Henry Geldzahler of the Metropolitan Museum. "Andy was pop and pop was Andy."[29]

New Directions

Building on his success as a painter of Pop Art, Warhol next decided to turn to sculpture.

With his preference for visible, everyday objects, he planned to use his silk-screening technique on plywood crates. He would create replicas of grocery boxes for Campbell's tomato juice, Kellogg's cornflakes, Del Monte peaches, Mott's apple juice, Heinz ketchup, and Brillo pads.[1] The idea was for the sculpture to resemble the originals in every way except that they would be nailed shut. Warhol envisioned four hundred boxes selling for $300 to $600 each.

Gerard Malanga, who had assisted Warhol previously in silk-screening projects, worked alongside the artist on the boxes. It was not easy. Each box required six handpainted sides. After the paint dried, four of the sides—and often all six of them—needed to be silk-screened. For his efforts, Malanga was paid $1.25 an hour, the minimum wage in New York at that time.[2]

The year was 1963 and Warhol had room in his studio for the project since he had recently moved his art supplies and equipment to an old hat factory on East Forty-seventh Street. The studio was about one hundred feet by fifty feet with a concrete floor. The windows along Forty-seventh Street faced south, but Warhol preferred keeping most of the light blocked out.[3] He stacked up the hundreds of plywood boxes along the walls. He called his studio the Factory, to play up the artist's assembly-line approach to his work. It took three months to complete the silk-screened crates.

The Brillo boxes were displayed at the Stable Gallery the following year in a show called—not surprisingly—"Brillo Boxes." Attendance was huge, with lines of people waiting for admission outside the gallery. The impact made by the boxes was sensational. But, as would often occur during Warhol's career, the show raised an important question: Was it really art? Warhol had often been accused of producing "empty" art. Were the hollow plywood boxes his response?[4]

"My favorite piece of sculpture is a solid wall with a hole in it to frame the space on the other side," Warhol said.[5]

Whether he was a Pop artist, a commercial artist, or an outright fraud, Warhol's fame continued to

Warhol turned to sculpture after becoming famous for his paintings. He painted wooden crates to look exactly like Brillo boxes and cartons of Heinz ketchup.

spread. Likewise, the phenomenon called Pop became a vital part of sixties culture, spreading from art to fashion to music.

"Once you 'got' Pop, you could never see a sign the same way again," Warhol said. "And once you thought Pop, you could never see America the same way again."[6]

While he was working on his grocery boxes, Warhol decided to try his hand at filmmaking. He worked on a movie called *Tarzan and Jane Revisited . . . Sort of,* a silent movie filmed with a sixteen-millimeter camera.

He went on to make *Sleep*, which was a six-hour film of stockbroker John Giorno sleeping. Warhol did nothing more in making this movie than focus a camera on Giorno and let the film run. *Sleep* was the first of Warhol's underground films—experimental movies he produced himself. Most viewers thought it was a waste of their time. Others, such as *Film Culture* magazine publisher Jonas Mekas, believed that Warhol was demonstrating a new vision of the world.[7]

Warhol continued making films. In *Kiss, Haircut,* and *Eat,* he simply set up a camera and let the film roll.

What was the purpose of making *Eat?* he was asked. Shot in black and white, the silent film showed a man eating a mushroom for forty-five minutes. "Well, it took him that long to eat one mushroom," Warhol explained. When asked why he thought it was necessary to film it, Warhol replied, "Uhhh, I don't know. He was there and he was eating a mushroom."[8]

Eventually, Warhol turned in the sixteen-millimeter camera for a thirty-five millimeter one. Then, he gradually added motion, music, talking, a script for dialogue, plot, and color.

"People usually just go to the movies to see only the star . . . ," Warhol said in explanation of these early films. "So here at least is a chance to look only at the star for as long as you like. . . . It was also easier to make."[9]

Warhol was developing a definite style—both for himself and for the Factory, where he spent most of his hours. He asked Billy Name, a hairdresser and theatrical lighting man, to turn the Factory into a completely silver studio. Using paint and aluminum foil, Name worked hard through the first four months of 1964, sleeping on the studio's floor when he grew tired. Finally, Name turned the entire Factory—floor, ceiling, furniture, and cabinets—silver.

"What I most remember about the Factory itself is the aluminum foil that covered the walls, and the stuffed couch," said Danny Fields, a magazine editor. "Stone floors, a lot of paintings, a lot of standing around, a movie projector and cans of film. Some Salvation Army furniture to sit on. . . . A coin wall telephone by the door . . . [and] a sign, DO NOT ENTER UNLESS YOU ARE EXPECTED, which everyone ignored."[10]

The Factory quickly became a hangout for artists and art collectors, millionaires and actors. Many of these people were drug users. Warhol himself continually took diet pills both to stay thin and to stay awake.

He was always concerned about his weight. "I did like to eat a lot . . . candy and very rare meat. I loved them both," he said. "Some days I'd just eat one or the other all day long."[11]

He claimed he slept only two or three hours each night from 1965 through 1967.[12]

He now dressed all in black—black stretch jeans, black T-shirt, pointed black boots, dark glasses—and he favored a silver wig to match the interior of the Factory. If he did not say much in public before, he said even less now. He rarely showed emotion and when he did speak, he talked in a monotone.[13] Often, at the end of an interview, he would say, "Have I lied enough?"[14]

Warhol was commissioned in 1964 to create a mural for the New York World's Fair. He submitted a black-and-white picture, twenty by twenty feet, titled *The Thirteen Most Wanted Men.* He had used photographs of criminals to make the picture, which was mounted on the exterior of the New York State pavilion. However, the governor of New York, Nelson Rockefeller, felt Warhol's work was offensive and wanted it removed. Warhol's response was simply to cover the enormous picture with silver paint.

During that summer, Warhol shot another movie, *Empire.* As with his other films, Warhol hardly touched the camera. He merely focused it on the Empire State Building from eight at night until two-thirty in the morning. The movie was shown at the Bridge Cinema, and most members of the audience either booed or threw objects at the screen. Yet several months later, Warhol won *Film Culture* magazine's award for contributions to film.

Warhol was not particularly interested in the audience's or critics' reactions to his work; he continued shooting movies. Edith Sedgwick—called Edie—became a star of his underground movies when she appeared in *Poor Little Rich Girl.* Using no script, Sedgwick simply talked about herself for more than an hour.

Ronald Tavel, who wrote several of Warhol's films, said the best way to work on these movies was "to work for no meaning. Which is pretty calculated in itself: you work at something so that it means nothing . . . my problem as the scriptwriter was to make the

In his 1964 movie Empire, *Warhol focused his camera on the* Empire State Building, *above, for several hours. Audiences booed and threw things at the screen, but* Film Culture *magazine gave Warhol an award.*

scripts so they meant nothing, no matter how they were approached."[15]

Warhol was still painting and had recently made the move from Eleanor Ward's Stable Gallery to the gallery owned by Leo Castelli. Listening to a friend's advice, he decided to make paintings based on lighter, less depressing subjects. Warhol silk-screened a photograph by Patricia Caulfield of four hibiscus flowers onto a green background. He made hundreds of paintings of the flowers, ranging in size from a few inches to twelve feet. The paintings sold out, and reviewers called the artist a genius, a saint, and a Renaissance man—someone with many interests and talents.

Warhol commented that the paintings looked "like a cheap awning."[16]

In 1965, Warhol traveled to Paris. Pop Art was extremely well received in France and his paintings of flowers were to be shown at the Sonnabend Gallery there. The show was an immediate success, breaking previous attendance records. Warhol was sought out for interviews; his photograph appeared in *Vogue* and *Paris-Match* magazines, two of the most widely read magazines in Europe.

During his stay in France, Warhol had announced that he was retiring from painting in order to turn all his attention to filmmaking. His motivation was not due to lack of interest in painting, but to boost the price of his work. Once an artist no longer produces new artwork, the paintings that exist are worth more money. Warhol planned to return to painting once the value of his pictures had increased.[17]

Warhol left Paris and headed to London, where again he was the target of the media. He then went on to Madrid and Tangiers before returning to New York.

His next project was to make the film *Kitchen*. Starring Edie Sedgwick, it contained more of a plot than any of his previous movies. Sedgwick sat at a kitchen table talking to two men and was killed at the end of the movie for no reason. Warhol commented that the film was "illogical, without motivation or character, and completely ridiculous. Very much like real life."[18]

Author Norman Mailer considered Warhol's films historical documents. "I suspect that a hundred years from now people will look at *Kitchen* and say, 'Yes, that's the way it was in the late Fifties, early Sixties in America. That's why they had the war in Vietnam. That's why the rivers were getting polluted.'"[19]

More movies followed *Kitchen*, and Warhol started to become something of a legend. He was idolized by young people throughout the world and had five fan clubs in the United States.

He and Sedgwick traveled to Philadelphia's Institute of Contemporary Art to attend Warhol's first American retrospective, an exhibition of his previous work. More than two thousand people showed up at the opening. The exhibit area was able to hold only seven hundred, and the museum was packed with fans screaming for their idol.

Warhol and Sedgwick were trapped on a flight of stairs in the building for at least two hours. People passed items to them to be autographed, such as shopping bags, candy wrappers, address books, train tickets, and soup cans.[20] Finally, police led the couple onto the roof of the building through a hole in the ceiling. They managed to climb down a fire escape and were driven away by police. The event further solidified Warhol's reputation as a star.

"I wondered what it was that had made all those people scream," Warhol wrote. "It was incredible to think of it happening at an *art* opening. Even a Pop Art opening. But then we weren't just *at* the art exhibit— we *were* the art exhibit."[21]

Warhol ventured into new territory at the close of 1965. Discotheques, or dance clubs, were popular at the time and Warhol now put together a multimedia club. It was located at a Polish dance hall on St. Mark's Place, called Stanley's the Dom.

At the club, Warhol used five movie projectors to show his films in the background, while strobe lights flashed on the enormous dance floor. Interpretative dancers ran about the place, and several slide projectors flashed different pictures on the walls every ten seconds. In the midst of this, the rock group the Velvet Underground performed. A huge mirrored ball hung from the ceiling, reflecting the activity below.

Lou Reed, a singer with the group, recalled a conversation with Warhol. "He said, 'Gee, I've got this week to do a show, and I was gonna show my movies, but why don't you play, and I'll show my movies on *you*?'" Reed recalled.[22]

Advertised as the Exploding Plastic Inevitable, the club made $18,000 during its first week. It appealed to everyone. People from different backgrounds and

Warhol, far left, with members of the rock band the Velvet Underground—Maureen Tucker, Sterling Morrison, and Lou Reed. In 1966, Warhol made a movie featuring the group.

interests—whether it was dance, music, art, fashion, or film—flocked to the Dom.

"He created multimedia in New York," Reed said. "All these clubs now with their lights and everything—they owe that mixed-media thing directly to Andy. The way people dress was affected by it, everything was affected by it. The whole complexion of the city changed, probably of the country. Nothing remained the same after that."[23]

At this time, Warhol decided to produce a record album of the Velvet Underground. Just as he kept a distance from the movies he made, Warhol allowed the musicians to do what they liked, essentially making the record themselves.

While the Exploding Plastic Inevitable club was operating, Warhol gave what would be his last show of new artwork for the next eleven years at the Castelli Gallery. One room of the gallery was covered with wallpaper containing cows' heads, similar to Elsie, the trademark cow for Borden's dairy. Another room held silver helium balloons that floated about.

The show attracted attention; it seemed as if anything that had Warhol's name associated with it became the subject of interest. Critics were confused but enthusiastic. Warhol, with his silver wig and expressionless gaze, remained closemouthed and detached.

Out of Control

"In the future everyone will be famous for fifteen minutes," Warhol once said.[1]

Yet the artist's fame was lasting considerably longer than his predicted fifteen minutes. During the summer of 1966, he began working on another film. *Chelsea Girls* would turn out to be one of his most successful movies ever, bridging the gap between underground and legitimate theaters.

In making *Chelsea Girls*, Warhol filmed scenes at the Factory, several apartments and the Chelsea Hotel on West Twenty-third Street. He shot a total of fifteen reels of film.

Typically, there was no plot to the movie. As for the "script," writer Ronald Tavel had sent a few rough sketches to Warhol. But the film basically revolved around focusing the camera on Warhol's friends and colleagues from the Factory. For thirty-five minutes at a stretch, the camera would focus on the actors, waiting for something to happen.

"This way I can catch people being themselves instead of . . . letting people act out parts that were written," Warhol said.[2]

The six-and-a-half-hour movie premiered on September 15 at the Cinematheque. Warhol was able to cut this time in half by using a split screen and showing two reels of film at the same time.

The movie was instantly successful, not just with the underground audience, but with the general public. Many reviews were also favorable, though some critics found Warhol's work totally offensive. Within two months, *Chelsea Girls* was being shown in some of New York's legitimate theaters. And it was a financial success as well. In only six months, it earned $300,000.

Warhol's increasing popularity in all areas of his career created many demands on his time. He often allowed people hanging around the Factory to answer the telephone in his place. They gave interviews to reporters as if *they* were Andy Warhol.[3]

In 1967, Warhol got into trouble when he allowed someone to impersonate him on a college lecture tour. Always nervous about speaking in public, Warhol usually traveled with several actors who had appeared in his films. They would speak to the audience and answer all the questions; Warhol would merely sit quietly onstage.

The day before Warhol was to leave on a lecture

tour out west, he commented that he did not feel like going. Allen Midgette, who had appeared in a few of Warhol's movies, suggested taking the artist's place. Warhol agreed. Midgette's hair was quickly sprayed silver before he traveled across the country to give lectures in Utah and Oregon.

Four months later, someone at one of the colleges noticed that a magazine photograph of Warhol did not match a photo taken of him while he was visiting the college. Warhol had no excuse, except to say it had "seemed like a good idea at the time."[4] Plus, Midgette

By the mid-1960s, Warhol was idolized by young people throughout the world.

was "more like what people expect than I could ever be," he said.[5]

The following year, Warhol's career took a decided turn. But this time, he had absolutely no control over it.

Warhol spent the morning of June 3, 1968, shopping at Bloomingdale's department store and meeting with his lawyer. By late afternoon, he had finished with his business and took a taxicab to the Factory. He entered the building with one of his assistants, Jed Johnson, and Valerie Solanas, who had appeared in one of Warhol's films.

Once inside the Factory, Warhol sat down at a desk. Solanas then reached into a brown bag she had been carrying, pulled out an automatic pistol, and fired. One of the bullets struck Warhol. It entered his right side and injured several internal organs before exiting through his left side. Solanas aimed next at art critic Mario Amaya. After wounding Amaya, Solanas threatened to shoot someone else, but the gun jammed. She got on the elevator and left the building.

Warhol was rushed to Cabrini Medical Center in an ambulance. He entered the emergency room at 4:45 P.M. in critical condition. Doctors operated for five and a half hours, removing Warhol's spleen, which had ruptured. Warhol continued to fight for his life over the next few days.

By his second week in the hospital, some of his friends were allowed to visit. Ten days after he had been admitted to the hospital, doctors declared Warhol would be able to make a complete recovery.

He stayed in the hospital for six weeks. During that time, he was given many gifts of cakes, candies, and other foods. Warhol was terrified that the food might be poisoned; he made sure his nephews sampled the food before he would eat it himself.[6]

Solanas had turned herself in on the night of the shooting. "He had too much control of my life," she said, later explaining that Warhol had promised to produce a screenplay she had written but had not yet done so. "I just wanted him to pay attention to me. Talking to him was like talking to a chair."[7]

Appearing in Manhattan Criminal Court, Solanas was determined to defend herself and not hire a lawyer. She also claimed to have no regrets about the shooting. She was later taken to the psychiatric ward at Bellevue Hospital for observation.

Solanas was indicted on charges of attempted murder, assault, and illegal possession of a gun. She was eventually declared incompetent to stand trial and was committed to a mental institution. A year later, Solanas was sentenced to three years in prison for reckless assault with intent to harm.[8]

Warhol was released from the hospital on July 28. He remained in bed for nearly two weeks watching television. His first public appearance took place on September 4, when he went to a restaurant in Greenwich Village. A reporter from the *Village Voice* asked him if he was still in pain. Warhol responded that the shooting had forced him to slow down his activities; he was not able to do everything he wanted to do.

"Since I was shot everything is such a dream to

me," he said. "I don't know whether or not I'm really alive—whether I died. It's sad. . . . Life is like a dream."[9]

The reporter asked Warhol if he was scared now. The artist admitted he was.

When Warhol returned to the Factory later that month, it was decided that an entrance hallway would be built in order to screen visitors. Warhol preferred to remain secluded in his office. Whenever he heard the elevator doors open, he would begin to shake.

But still, the Factory remained full of an odd assortment of people. Although Warhol was now afraid of them, he was even more afraid of losing them. He worried that if he was no longer surrounded by "crazy" people "jabbering away and doing their insane things," he would lose his creativity.[10]

But he *was* managing without them. In fact, the value of his paintings had skyrocketed from $200 to $15,000 since the shooting.

Making films continued to be Warhol's main area of interest. "The best atmosphere I can think of is film," he wrote, "because it's three-dimensional physically and two-dimensional emotionally."[11]

Through 1969, he worked on his movies, explaining that he preferred not to use scripts because they bored him. He found it was more interesting not to know how the story would develop.

"It's much more exciting not to know what's going to happen," he said. "*This is my favorite theme in moviemaking*—just watching something happening for two hours or so. . . . we're real people trying not to say anything."[12]

In 1968, the Factory moved to the sixth floor of this building at 33 Union Square West. Photos of 1930s movie stars and Warhol superstars decorated the white walls.

He stuck to this theme when writing the novel *a* in the summer of 1969. The book was based on tapes made about the daily life of Robert Olivo, a Factory groupie who called himself Ondine. Just as Warhol's movies seemed to be mere segments of life with no beginning, middle, or end, so was *a*. Warhol and his assistants also made sure that nothing in the book was edited. He wanted every grammatical error, spelling mistake, and typographical error to be included. He wanted to make a bad book, he said, just as he had made bad movies and bad art. He liked "bad" and he liked "boring."[13]

The book went on sale for $10 and generally received poor reviews. Warhol had been hoping it would be turned into a movie. Still, he was very pleased with it. It was different; nothing like it had been done before. He claimed to have read it forty times.[14]

The Art of Business

"**W**hat was he impressed with, then?" wrote Pat Hackett, one of Warhol's assistants, about the artist. "Fame . . . old, new, or faded. Beauty. Classical talent. Innovative talent. Anyone who did anything *first*. A certain kind of outrageous nerve. Good talkers. Money. . . . He never took his success for granted; he was thrilled to have it."[1]

Since the shooting, Warhol had become even more successful; the value of his paintings steadily increased. With this in mind, his assistants at the Factory planned a retrospective exhibit of his work in 1970. The show would open in Pasadena, California, and then move on to Chicago, the Netherlands, Paris, London, and New York. It would consist of the artist's various series, including the soup cans, Brillo boxes, disaster paintings, flowers, and portraits.

Warhol's involvement in selecting the works for the show was minimal.

"I like empty walls," he commented. "As soon as you put something on them they look terrible."[2]

The retrospective opened at the Pasadena Museum in May 1970. The day after the opening, one of Warhol's paintings was purchased for $60,000. No living American artist had ever received a higher price for his work.[3]

When the show moved to Musee d'Art Moderne in Paris in November, it was termed a "great event."[4] The reaction in London was equally positive when the show opened at the Tate Gallery. Throughout Europe, Warhol was treated like a major celebrity. Students chased him down streets, hoping for his autograph, and those attending the retrospective show were disappointed when they were unable to catch a glimpse of the artist.

The Whitney Museum in New York hosted the retrospective on April 26, 1971. Warhol had dropped his distant manner for this show and consulted everyone around him about whether to cover the walls of the museum with his cow wallpaper.

"That's how Andy worked," said Bob Colacello, a magazine writer. "He would ask almost everyone he met what he should do, what he should paint, what colors he should use, what film he should do, what Superstars he should use, as if he were taking a poll, and then he would do exactly what *he* wanted to do."[5]

In the end, Warhol decided to cover the walls with

green and magenta wallpaper, decorated with his cow design. Over the wallpaper, his paintings hung as large as billboards. The enormous space on the museum's fourth floor was filled with Warhol's serial paintings of Marilyn Monroe, Campbell's soup cans, car crashes, electric chairs, and flowers.

Attendance at the museum was tremendous. The only time a larger crowd had come to the museum was for American artist Andrew Wyeth's show four years earlier. Warhol's opening night was filled with television cameras, flashbulbs, and microphones. Warhol joked with one art critic that he planned on changing his name to John Doe because he had become too famous.[6]

As the retrospective drew to a close, Warhol returned to filmmaking. He traveled to Los Angeles that summer to film *Heat*, which was based on the movie *Sunset Boulevard*. The story revolves around an aging movie star who tries to recapture the fame of her youth. Warhol also began spending a considerable amount of time with various celebrities, including rock stars. He even designed the cover for the Rolling Stones' *Sticky Fingers* album. Now Warhol wore velvet jackets in place of leather and carried his miniature dachshund Archie around with him.

Warhol had asked his brother Paul to take care of their mother. Julia Warhola was nearly eighty years old. She had suffered a stroke and was also losing her memory. While staying with Paul in Pittsburgh, she had another stroke. It was decided to put her into a nursing home. Andy Warhol always made it a point to call his mother on a regular basis, but he never saw

The Whitney Museum in New York City hosted a retrospective of Warhol's work in 1971.

her again. She died in November 1972. Warhol did not attend the funeral.

Forever bouncing back and forth between film-making and painting, Warhol decided to again focus on painting. Most of Warhol's paintings by this time were special requests. His next assignment was for Democrats who supported George McGovern in the 1972 presidential election. Instead of using McGovern's image in the *Vote McGovern* series, Warhol did a portrait of the senator's opponent, President Richard Nixon. But he painted Nixon in grotesque colors—green face, yellow mouth—and the pictures raised $40,000 for McGovern's campaign.

Ever since the retrospective show, Warhol's pictures had been increasing in value. European art dealer Bruno Bischofberger suggested that Warhol paint the most important figure of the twentieth century. Bischofberger instructed his staff to go through history books, and they determined that Albert Einstein was the most important man of the century. But Warhol had recently seen an article in *Life* magazine stating that Mao Tse-tung, the revolutionary leader who founded the People's Republic of China, was the most famous person in the world. Warhol intended to paint Mao.[7]

Over a three-month period in 1972, he worked on more than two thousand paintings of Mao. With works ranging from six inches to seventeen feet, the series included handpainted brushstrokes on the paintings as well as numerous rolls of Mao wallpaper done in purple and white.

The Mao series was put on display in Paris in February 1974. As always, the Europeans were wildly enthusiastic about Warhol's work. They considered him the most important artist in America, the most serious artist alive. The Mao series was greeted with equal enthusiasm in New York. They were paintings about power, but they were also commercial and controversial.[8]

In between painting and making films about Dracula and Frankenstein, Warhol started an underground monthly magazine called *Interview*. The first editor was Rosemary Kent of *Women's Wear Daily*. But when she and Warhol found they did not work well together, Bob Colacello was brought in to edit the magazine. For the first several years, *Interview* made little money and Warhol thought about stopping publication.

But instead of dropping the magazine, it was decided to change its focus. Originally, it had been a movie magazine written by poets and artists. Now it would concentrate on entertainment and fashion, appealing to celebrities and fashion-conscious readers. It would be a reflection of the world in which Warhol lived.

Interview set the trend for the stylish magazines that were so popular during the 1980s. In addition to celebrity photographs, *Interview* included celebrity interviews often conducted by Warhol. Still relying on natural, spontaneous behavior, Warhol would bring his tape recorder to his interviews, turn it on, and let it run. The interview was then printed practically word for word, including Warhol's end of the conversation. Typically, Warhol wanted the magazine to be a combination of bad and boring.

"Why do you have to spend so much time proof-reading?" he would complain to his editors.[9]

The new format was a success. In six months, the circulation more than doubled, reaching seventy-four thousand. The money received from advertisements also climbed. According to Pat Hackett, Warhol's secretary, it was the magazine that prevented Warhol from "passing into sixties history."[10] Because of *Interview*, Warhol continued to meet new, creative people who kept his own creativity alive.

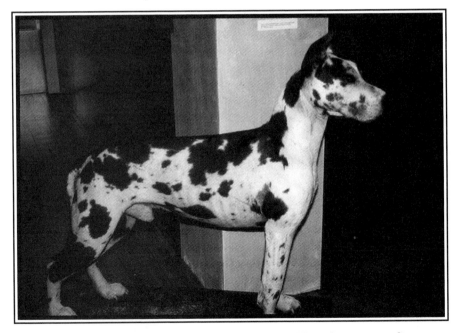

Andy made the art he wanted to create, and his ideas were often offbeat—like "Cecil" the stuffed Great Dane, who stood guard at the Factory.

By this time, Warhol had turned his business into a company, Andy Warhol Enterprises. He enlarged his office space by renting a 12,500-square-foot suite of rooms located at 860 Broadway in August 1974. Warhol went to work making prints and appearing in advertisements in order to earn money for the high rental fees. He told his receptionists not to answer the phone with "Factory," but to call it "the Office."[11]

Dividing his time among filmmaking, painting, and the magazine, Warhol met with celebrities and business prospects over lunch each day, then generally spent the afternoon painting. His portrait business was booming. He routinely charged $25,000 for a picture that measured forty inches by forty inches.

His technique for creating portraits was complicated. First, Warhol would use his Polaroid camera to take instant photographs of the subject. He would sometimes demand more than one session and often took sixty photos to obtain what he was looking for. Warhol's aim was to end up with a photo that had a considerable amount of graphic contrast—a lot of light and dark tones.

He would then go to work on a forty-by-forty-inch negative (which was the standard portrait size) with a pair of scissors. He would cut away any of the subject's imperfections—double chins, bags under the eyes, bumps in the nose. He would remove wrinkles from the neck. Although various people contributed in the making of these portraits, only Warhol worked on the negatives.[12]

The proof was traced onto the canvas and Warhol then added background colors. Eyes, lips, and other facial features would be painted in before giving the canvas to a printer who silk-screened the black-and-white image onto the canvas. The final stage included actual brushwork by Warhol onto the silk screen.

In his portraits as in his other work, Warhol carefully removed himself from his art as much as possible. Not only did he use the mechanical process of silk-screening, but he even hired assistants to do the work for him.

As always, he remained mysteriously quiet about his work. Henry Geldzahler, of the Metropolitan Museum of Art, once quizzed Warhol, "Do you know what you are doing?"

"No," the artist replied.

Did he know what a painting would look like before starting actual work on it?

"No."

Did his paintings usually turn out as he expected?

"No."

Did that surprise him?

"No," answered Warhol.[13]

Warhol worked every day of the week, and he was getting paid handsomely for his efforts. But no matter how much he earned, his childhood years had left him with a fear of being poor. Rather than carrying credit cards, Warhol liked to be aware of how much money he was spending. He walked around with a brown envelope that contained several hundred-dollar bills.[14]

As for his portrait commissions, Warhol never hid the fact that they were an easy way for him to make money.

"Business art is the step that comes after Art," he wrote. "I started as a commercial artist, and I want to finish as a business artist . . . making money is art and working is art and good business is the best art."[15]

Famous Faces

Warhol's daily routine in the mid-seventies had little variation until the day he died. In the morning, he would dictate his diary—which was published in 1989—over the telephone to Pat Hackett. Then he would take his dachshunds, Archie and Amos, into the kitchen (three flights below his bedroom) and have breakfast. This was followed by a few hours of shopping, an important part of Warhol's day.

"He was a massive shopper," said Frederick Hughes, a longtime friend of the artist's. "He considered shopping a part of his work, and every day he bought things that caught his eye on his rounds of flea markets and antique stores, anything from nineteenth-century sculpture and furniture to tiny little collectibles, like World's Fair items."[1]

While shopping, Warhol would hand out copies of *Interview* magazine to shopkeepers, hoping they would place advertisements in it. Arriving at the Factory, he would go through his mail, placing certain letters, invitations, gifts, and magazines into a time capsule. These capsules were brown cardboard boxes measuring ten inches by eighteen inches by fourteen inches. Once items were placed inside the box, it was sealed, dated, and stored. Another box would then replace it.[2]

He would eat lunch with clients at the Factory and paint for the remainder of the afternoon. His evenings were spent attending various dinners, parties, and openings in hopes of finding more clients for portraits. He went to church on Sundays, and about once a month he would travel to Europe, Hollywood, or Washington, D.C., to break up the routine.[3]

Some art critics claim that Warhol's talent never recovered from the shooting the decade before. Others disagree. In any case, the artist continued looking for new creative outlets.[4] After successfully entering the worlds of art, film, music, and publishing, he next became involved in producing a Broadway musical.

Man on the Moon starred John Phillips, the singer who had once led the pop group the Mamas and the Papas. His wife, actress Genevieve Waite, was also involved in the show. Created by Paul Morrissey, who had been working with Warhol since the mid-sixties, *Man on the Moon* was a failure. After opening on January 29, 1975, the show closed three days later.

"Making money is art and working is art and good business is the best art," said Warhol. His large office space at 860 Broadway, above, housed his art studios and Interview *magazine.*

Morrissey moved to Hollywood, and Warhol turned his attention back to his portrait painting.

He now spent a significant amount of time in Germany, where he was hired to paint portraits of wealthy German citizens. During this time, Dr. Erich Marx, a major German collector of contemporary art, decided to acquire the largest collection of Warhol paintings in the world. The result of this action was to boost the value of Warhol's works even higher. Starting with some handpainted advertisements Warhol had created at the start of his career, Marx eventually collected more than twenty canvases.

Warhol was also working on several portraits of rock star Mick Jagger. The paintings were to be signed by both the artist and the musician.

The portraits that were produced between 1975 and 1976 had a similar soft look. They were painted in pastel colors, such as lavender and light green, and the subject generally had a faraway look in the eyes. Warhol painted several portraits of Jagger, assuming the rock star was wealthy enough to buy all of them or that his fame would make him a profitable subject. Jagger, however, purchased only the three most flattering portraits.[5]

Warhol's star continued to rise. In May, he was invited to dinner at the White House by President Gerald Ford. Always shy, Warhol was extremely nervous about his first visit there. He dyed one eyebrow white and the other black, carefully put on a wig, and doused himself heavily with a homemade fragrance. He wore a white tie and a formal white jacket and

Warhol's images of Marilyn Monroe helped make him famous in the early 1960s. Later in his career, he painted many portraits of celebrities as an easy way to make money.

pants, with blue jeans underneath the dress pants because they were itchy.[6]

In 1975, Warhol published a book containing his thoughts on various aspects of life. Based on tapes of his telephone conversations, *The Philosophy of Andy Warhol: From A to B and Back Again* was labeled "negative philosophy" by its author.[7] To the critics, it was considered a book that represented life in America in the 1970s. The book was a compilation of Warhol's theories on such topics as work, beauty, death, and fame. The chapter on death consists of forty-six words. Warhol wrote that he believed everything was "magic" and that death would never happen.[8]

Warhol began a book-signing tour of nine cities in

the United States. Everywhere, the response was enthusiastic and he enjoyed himself as well. In Houston, Warhol and Ann Lambton, one of his assistants, stood in a department store window and pretended to be mannequins. While they posed, music by the Velvet Underground played loudly in the background. He sold a minimum of one hundred fifty books at each signing and occasionally sold double that number over a course of two hours. He gave interviews in each city, although he considered them "torture." The question he most dreaded was "Are you rich?" For an answer, Warhol would often point to his shoes, which were splattered with paint.

After the United States tour, he headed to Europe. There he attended book parties and art openings in Italy, France, and England.

When he returned from Europe, Warhol moved into a five-story mansion on the Upper East Side of Manhattan. The house quickly filled with the artist's vast number of collectibles: busts of Napoleon, Lafayette, and Benjamin Franklin; Chippendale sofas and Art Deco chairs; works of art by Picasso, Edvard Munch, Jasper Johns, and Roy Lichtenstein; rare books; ornate urns; bronze statues of horses, dogs, and dancers.

Although Warhol's treasures were worth millions of dollars, he still kept money stuffed under his mattress, which was made especially for him of straw. Rarely entertaining in his new home because it made him so uncomfortable, Warhol kept most of the rooms locked. He spent his time mainly in the kitchen and the bedroom.

"He had a routine," said his assistant Jed Johnson. "He'd walk through the house every morning before he left, open the door of each room with a key, peer in, then re-lock it. Then at night when he came home he would unlock each door, turn the light on, peer in, lock up, and go to bed."[9]

In 1976, Warhol began working with American painter James Wyeth. Wyeth was the son of Andrew Wyeth, an American artist widely known for his portraits and stark paintings of farms and landscapes, and the grandson of N. C. Wyeth, whose richly painted illustrations transformed the nature of that genre. Like his father, James Wyeth is well known for his portraits as well as his earthy paintings of animals and farms in Maine and Pennsylvania.

The Coe-Kerr Gallery in New York had commissioned Wyeth and Warhol to paint each other's portraits. Although the two artists had vastly different styles of painting, Warhol thought the collaboration would be good for his image. At the very least, it would link his name with a painter who was considered a serious American artist in the traditional sense.

The Coe-Kerr show was held in June and included the original drawings the artists had made before actually starting the portraits. It was a huge success and received good reviews.

The friendship between the artists endured, and Warhol invited Wyeth to work on his own projects at the Factory. Wyeth took him up on his offer, painting portraits that included bodybuilder and actor Arnold Schwarzenegger.

The New York Times Magazine asked Warhol to

paint a portrait of Democratic presidential candidate Jimmy Carter for its cover. Traveling to Georgia, Warhol took photographs of Carter. He later described the future president as "really quiet." The family member he liked best was Carter's mother, Miss Lillian, because she kept telling Warhol she looked like him.[10] The magazine cover ran on September 26, 1976, and Warhol eventually made one hundred prints of the portrait to help raise funds for Carter's campaign. Carter, who grew up on a peanut farm in Plains, Georgia, thanked the artist for the portrait by giving him two signed bags of peanuts.[11]

In 1977, Warhol had a major show. It was a series of paintings based on the symbol of the Communist Party, the hammer and sickle. Warhol photographed a mallet and sickle from a nearby hardware store and then made the photos into a silk screen. In a slight variation of his previous works, Warhol used a sponge mop to apply broad strokes of paint to the canvas. The exhibit was held in January at Leo Castelli's gallery in New York and later opened in Belgium.

That year, Warhol created another album cover for the Rolling Stones and enjoyed inviting rock groups such as Talking Heads, Blondie, and The Clash to the Factory. He also began spending most of his evenings at Studio 54, a disco club that had recently opened in New York. Warhol quickly became one of the names associated with the club, along with fashion designer Halston, celebrity Bianca Jagger, and actress Liza Minnelli. He brought his tape recorder and camera to the club, where famous and powerful people gathered

Warhol, right, was invited to a White House reception with President Jimmy Carter, left. The New York Times Magazine *had asked Warhol to paint a portrait of Jimmy Carter in 1976, during his election campaign.*

each night. When he would return home at six in the morning, Warhol would carefully put away his tapes.

Warhol traveled to Europe that spring for two purposes: his book *Andy Warhol's Philosophy* had been published in France, and his *Hammer and Sickle* series was opening at Gallerie D in Brussels, Belgium. As usual, he was mobbed by the Europeans, who demanded his autograph and viewed Warhol enthusiastically as the man who invented punk rock.

In fact, Warhol put together a punk rock act when he returned to the United States. Walter Steding, an electric violinist who was also one of Warhol's painting assistants, performed at a New York punk rock club. Warhol produced a record by Steding, but nothing more came of the violinist's career.

In June 1977, Warhol was asked to take part in a White House reception honoring several contemporary artists, including Robert Rauschenberg, Roy Lichtenstein, and James Wyeth. Warhol renewed his friendship with President Carter's mother, Miss Lillian, and even took her to a party at Studio 54. He painted her portrait later in the year.

He was especially busy now painting the portraits of well-known athletes. Creating a total of six portraits of each athlete, he gave one to the subject and put the other five up for sale. Sitting for Warhol were Muhammad Ali, O. J. Simpson, Chris Evert, Pelé, Tom Seaver, Dorothy Hamill, Willie Shoemaker, and Kareem Abdul-Jabbar.

A year later, Warhol began developing ideas for television, and his shows aired from 1979 to 1987. One had a spontaneous format similar to that of his magazine, *Interview*. This program, called *Andy Warhol's TV*, consisted of thirty-minute talks with wealthy and famous individuals.

"He became famous in every field he entered," said Tina Fredericks. "Even though most people are not sure exactly what Andy was famous *for*, his name permeates our culture."[12]

His other television programs featured fashion shows and visits with stars at their homes. In many ways, Warhol's ideas paved the way for the music videos that would be so popular in the 1980s.

Falling

Warhol was a workaholic. He was never able to relax and had always hated vacations. He dreaded having time on his hands and had an unflagging desire to keep making money.[1]

While his portraits continued to bring in money, Warhol felt it was time to come up with something new. It had been three years since he had shown anything original at a gallery.

The artist had always been fascinated by the corners of his canvases, the area where the images of the silk screen began to disappear and all that remained was a series of dots. He decided to do paintings based on images of shadows. Shown at New York's Heiner Friedrich Gallery in 1979, these shadow paintings were abstract works and more serious than much of

Although his work was always controversial, Warhol was considered a pioneer of Pop Art.

his artwork. The paintings were sold out before they were displayed at the gallery.

By now, Warhol was fifty-one. His next move was to turn publisher with Andy Warhol Books, an imprint of Grosset and Dunlap Publishers. He published *Andy Warhol's Exposures*, which consisted of his Polaroid photographs of celebrities along with some gossipy text. The pictures were all black and white and not particularly flattering. Sales were poor even though Warhol embarked on a tour of twenty-five American and European cities. Only a collector's edition, which was decorated in gold and included a signed lithograph, sold fairly well at $500.

Meanwhile, more than fifty of Warhol's portraits went on display that fall at the Whitney Museum in New York City. It would be Warhol's final major exhibition of the decade. Mao Tse-tung, Sylvester Stallone, Warhol's mother, and numerous other famous faces hung in the New York museum.

Some critics called the works shallow, even boring, and the majority of the reviews were negative. Warhol refused to defend himself when asked what he thought about a critic's comment that the paintings were awful. "He's right," answered the artist, chewing on a stick of gum.[2]

More than fifty portraits were hung in pairs in the museum, except for eight paintings of the artist's mother. The portraits of Julia Warhola had a more authentic look to them than the treatment Warhol gave his other subjects.[3] He used quick brush strokes to retouch the background and clothing, creating a haunting atmosphere.

Nearly all Warhol's portraits were a reflection of the most powerful and famous people of his age. Although art critics did not think highly of the Whitney show, Warhol's portrait business rose to new heights as a result of it.

Another series of paintings in the winter of 1980 did little to improve Warhol's standing in the art world. Returning to paintings he had produced almost two decades earlier—Marilyn Monroe, flowers, the Mona Lisa—Warhol reversed the silk-screening process so that negative images, rather than positive ones, were used. As a result, the paintings were essentially black. Again, critics found the works boring.

Several months later, Warhol came out with another book, *POPism*. Spanning the decade of the sixties, *POPism* represented the artist's own view of Pop culture in New York.

Searching for a way to burst back into the art world, Warhol had a show at the Castelli Gallery in 1982. A series of paintings of dollar signs made up the exhibit. It was a complete failure; not one painting sold.

Warhol was determined to cover new ground. On

A special exhibit at the opening of the Andy Warhol Museum in Pittsburgh in 1994 was the "Rain Machine" of constantly flowing water, which was placed in front of some of Warhol's flower paintings.

commission, he painted *Ten Portraits of Jews of the Twentieth Century.* The series included Sigmund Freud, Albert Einstein, George Gershwin, and the Marx Brothers. In another series, he used photographs of German stadiums and war monuments on which to base a series of paintings. He also painted his own version of art masterpieces such as Sandro Botticelli's *Birth of Venus,* a lyrical work done during the Italian Renaissance, and Norwegian artist Edvard Munch's haunting painting *The Scream.*

By this time, the Factory had moved yet again. The offices and studios now took up an entire block from East Thirty-second Street to East Thirty-third Street between Madison and Fifth Avenues. Both his magazine and cable TV show were doing well, and Warhol frequently appeared in television advertisements for such companies as Sony, New York Air, and Coca-Cola. By October 1984, Warhol's wealth was estimated at $20 million.

Plagued by fears of being unable to come up with something new, Warhol began working with a young artist named Jean-Michel Basquiat. Basquiat, who came from Brooklyn, had originally started creating art in New York's subways. Warhol was one of his idols, and they first met at the Factory in 1981. Warhol was unsure of Basquiat—who was rough looking—until the younger man's canvases began selling for $10,000 to $20,000.

Bruno Bischofberger came up with the idea that Basquiat and Warhol trade portraits. They each took several Polaroid shots of the other, and in about two hours, Basquiat returned with the finished picture.

Warhol had not even selected which photograph to use.[4]

Warhol was on his way to painting seriously again. From 1984 through 1985, the two artists worked together on a series of pictures. The Warhol-Basquiat show opened in the fall of 1985 at the Tony Shafrazi Gallery. The paintings were a combination of Basquiat's urban stick figures mixed with Warhol's corporate logos.[5] Art critics wrote that Basquiat had sacrificed his integrity in doing the series. The reviews convinced Basquiat that he should not work any longer with Warhol, and the relationship between the two ended.

Warhol traveled to California in 1985. He appeared as himself in an episode of the television show *The Loveboat*, and filmed a commercial for Diet Coke. He also painted a portrait of actress Lana Turner.

But financially successful as the trip was, Warhol remained unhappy. Ever since Basquiat's departure, he had been bored.[6] Nothing seemed to interest him, and when asked how his painting was going, he invariably responded that it was terrible. Although he still enjoyed seeing and being seen with celebrities, such as Madonna, Sean Penn, Bob Dylan, and Sting, he now spent many evenings at home alone. Often, he occupied himself at night by sitting in front of a large mirror and trying on some of his four hundred wigs.

"I don't think Uncle Andy was very happy at all, even with all that money and fame," commented Warhol's nephew George.[7]

A show of Warhol's self-portraits opened in July 1986 at the Anthony d'Offay Gallery in London.

Always a favorite with the Europeans, Warhol was considered a cultural hero, and people wept as he entered the gallery.

The self-portraits were based on photographs of Warhol sitting directly in front of the camera with his eyes wide open and his expression typically blank. Some of the portraits were silk-screened onto a pattern of military camouflage, creating a mysterious effect as it concealed much of the artist's face. The partially obscured image of Warhol's face seemed an accurate reflection of the artist's hidden personality.

"I paint pictures of myself to remind myself that I'm still around," he said.[8]

Six months later, Warhol had an extremely successful show at the Robert Miller Gallery in New York. He had created fine-print photographs that used four to twelve repetitions of a particular image. Some photos featured a fan of James Dean wearing a T-shirt with Dean's picture on it, while others were self-portraits. Reviews were excellent, and enormous crowds attended the show.

Warhol had numerous commissions at this time. He did a series of Reigning Queens for an Amsterdam gallery and another series of Frederick the Greats for a German art dealer. A gallery in Los Angeles wanted ninety-nine paintings of Campbell's soup boxes, and he was also commissioned to paint the Mercedes cars for the Daimler-Benz Corporation.

At the start of 1987, Warhol's photographs were exhibited at the Robert Miller Gallery. The crowd was so huge that Warhol hid behind a desk, giving autographs. The black-and-white photos covered

At the Andy Warhol Museum in Pittsburgh, Warhol's self-portraits can be seen from the street outside the museum through a window.

everything from flowered wallpaper to portraits of Lana Turner and Brooke Shields to the Washington Monument. The photos were hung in groups of four, six, nine, and twelve and were sewn together with bits of thread dangling from the seams. Reviews were excellent and the show was an artistic triumph for Warhol.[9]

When Warhol flew to Milan, Italy, later that winter of 1987, he would be attending his last show. He had created his own version of Leonardo da Vinci's masterpiece *The Last Supper*, using advertising logos such as General Electric and Dove soap, to make the work his own. Again, huge crowds of people came to the opening, but Warhol would have little time to enjoy the success. He was unable to leave his hotel in Milan near the end of his stay because he was experiencing a great deal of pain in his abdomen.

He did fly to Zurich, Switzerland, but returned to New York earlier than he had planned. By February, the pains in his stomach were so severe he was confined to his bed.

Warhol's problem was gallstones. Not only had he been suffering from them since the previous year, but now they had become enlarged and potentially life threatening. Also, his gallbladder was infected and he was advised to have it removed immediately. Warhol had feared hospitals ever since he had been shot, and he refused to have his gallbladder problem taken care of.

By the end of the week, he had no choice. The operation was scheduled, and surgery was performed on the morning of February 21. The operation went well, and there were no complications. Warhol spent the evening in his hospital room watching television.

The following morning, Warhol's private nurse found the artist had turned blue and had a weak pulse. Although a cardiac arrest team tried to resuscitate him, they were not successful. Warhol died February 22, 1987.

Warhol was buried wearing a pair of his sunglasses. His grave is in Pittsburgh, next to his parents' graves. He had once said that he only hoped to be remembered as a soup can. But Warhol's legacy goes beyond that. According to William Rubin, director of the Department of Painting and Sculpture at New York's Museum of Modern Art, "Andy Warhol was a serious artist whose posture was unseriousness. He was a pioneer of . . . pop art."[10]

Called the Prince of Pop, Warhol is generally considered the most influential American artist of our time.[11]

He was, perhaps, also one of the wealthiest.

In spite of the bland personality he showed to the world, Warhol was a shrewd businessman. "He was his own corporation," said a friend. "He traveled a lot, but he never enjoyed it. Every night he'd call the Factory, sometimes waking members of his staff up, to discuss the day's business."[12]

Warhol's will directed that the majority of his estate be used to establish a foundation "for the advancement of the visual arts."[13] And the estate was a large one. It was originally estimated at $20 million, but the figure was increased to $100 million when the paintings, real estate—worth about $4 million—and all his collections were considered. One cookie jar collection alone sold for $250,000 at an auction at Sotheby's in April 1988.[14]

Warhol had a large collection of works by famous nineteenth- and twentieth-century artists, including Delacroix and Picasso, Rauschenberg and Johns. He also had an enormous folk art collection and numerous pieces of nineteenth- and early-twentieth-century furniture.

Warhol's career included painting, writing, magazine publishing, filmmaking, television, and photography. One of the projects left unfinished at his death was a series of paintings entitled "The History of American TV." The ten important moments in television history were to include the 1969 walk on the moon, an interview with Marilyn Monroe by newsman Edward R. Murrow, and the appearance of the rock group the Beatles on the Ed Sullivan show.

Throughout his lifetime, Warhol was always controversial. He was called a genius . . . and he was called a joke. He was accused of merely being famous for being famous. His work was puzzling, and the artist himself was a mystery.

"If you want to know all about Andy Warhol," he once said, "just look at the surface: of my paintings and films and me, and there I am. There's nothing behind it."[15]

1928—Born Andy Warhola in Pittsburgh, Pennsylvania, on August 6.

1945—Enters Carnegie Institute of Technology.

1949—Travels to New York City and is hired as a commercial artist by *Glamour* magazine.

1952—Has his first gallery opening with "Fifteen Drawings Based on the Writings of Truman Capote."

1962—His paintings of Campbell's soup cans go on display and Pop Art takes root in the United States.

1963—Moves into the Factory at East Forty-seventh Street; makes the films *Tarzan and Jane Revisited . . . Sort of; Eat; Haircut;* and *Sleep.*

1964—Makes the film *Empire.*

1965—Opens his multimedia discotheque called the Exploding Plastic Inevitable.

1968—Is shot by Valerie Solanas, who claims Warhol has too much control over her life.

1969—Begins publishing *Interview* magazine.

1971—Major retrospective of Warhol's work opens at the Pasadena Museum.

1974—Series of paintings of Mao Tse-tung opens in Paris.

1975—His Broadway show, *Man on the Moon,* runs for three days; publishes *The Philosophy of Andy Warhol: From A to B and Back Again.*

1976—Begins working with American artist James Wyeth.

1977—Opens first major show of new work in ten years featuring his hammer and sickle paintings; honored at White House reception.

1979—Exhibits his shadow paintings at New York's Heiner Friedrich Gallery.

1984—Begins working with artist Jean-Michel Basquiat.

1986—Opens a show of his self-portraits in London.

1987—Dies of a heart attack on February 22, after having surgery.

Chapter 1. A Can of Soup

1. Victor Bockris, *The Life and Death of Andy Warhol* (New York: Bantam Books, 1989), p. 70.

2. Douglas C. McGill, "Andy Warhol, Pop Artist, Dies," *The New York Times*, February 23, 1987, p. A16.

3. Carter Ratcliff, *Andy Warhol* (New York: Abbeville Press, 1983), p. 20.

4. Bockris, p. 105.

5. John Coplans, *Andy Warhol* (Greenwich, Conn.: New York Graphic Society, 1970), p. 12.

6. Marco Livingstone, *Pop Art: A Continuing History* (New York: Harry N. Abrams, Inc., 1990), p. 77.

7. John Rublowsky, *Pop Art* (New York: Basic Books, Inc., 1965), p. 112.

8. Bockris, p. 115.

9. Ibid., p. 110.

10. Bob Colacello, *Holy Terror: Andy Warhol Close Up* (New York: HarperCollins Publishers, 1990), p. 28.

11. Richard Leslie, *Pop Art: A New Generation of Style* (New York: Todtri Productions Limited, 1997), p. 58.

12. Coplans, p. 13.

13. Kynaston McShine, editor, *Andy Warhol: A Retrospective* (New York: Museum of Modern Art, 1989), p. 457.

14. Bockris, p. 117.

15. Jose Maria Faerna, general editor, *Warhol* (New York: Harry N. Abrams, Inc., 1997), p. 23.

Chapter 2. Pittsburgh

1. Stefan Lorant, *Pittsburgh: The Story of an American City* (Lenox, Mass.: R.R. Donnelley & Sons Company, 1964), p. 288.

2. Ibid., p. 191.

3. Bob Colacello, *Holy Terror: Andy Warhol Close Up* (New York: HarperCollins Publishers, 1990), p. 12.

4. Ibid.

5. Victor Bockris, *The Life and Death of Andy Warhol* (New York: Bantam Books, 1989), p. 9.

6. John Coplans, *Andy Warhol* (Greenwich, Conn.: New York Graphic Society, 1970), p. 8.

7. Ibid.

8. Colacello, p. 15.

9. Bockris, p. 18.

10. Jeanne Marie Laskas, "A Tale of Two Brothers: One Is Andy Warhol, the Other Wishes He Were," *Life*, December 1989, p. 90.

11. Andy Warhol, *The Philosophy of Andy Warhol: From A to B and Back Again* (New York: Harcourt Brace Jovanovich, 1975), p. 22.

12. Ibid., p. 117.

13. Laskas, p. 90.

14. Colacello, p. 18.

15. Bockris, pp. 29–30.

16. Warhol, p. 22.

Chapter 3. College

1. Victor Bockris, *The Life and Death of Andy Warhol* (New York: Bantam Books, 1989), p. 36.

2. Bennard B. Perlman, "Ageless Andy Warhol," *The New York Times*, February 28, 1987, p. A31.

3. Bockris, p. 35.

4. Bob Colacello, *Holy Terror: Andy Warhol Close Up* (New York: HarperCollins Publishers, 1990), p. 19.

5. Ibid., p. 18.

6. Bockris, p. 39.

7. Colacello, p. 19.

8. Ibid.

9. Ibid., p. 20.

Chapter 4. New York

1. Jesse Kornbluth, *Pre-Pop Warhol* (New York: Random House, 1988), p. 10.

2. Ibid., p. 11.

3. Ibid.

4. Ibid., p. 12.

5. Ibid.

6. Ibid.

7. Ibid., p. 93.

8. Kurt Loder, "Andy Warhol: 1928-1987," *Rolling Stone*, April 9, 1987, p. 34.

9. Bob Colacello, *Holy Terror: Andy Warhol Close Up* (New York: HarperCollins Publishers, 1990), p. 22.

10. Victor Bockris, *The Life and Death of Andy Warhol* (New York: Bantam Books, 1989), p. 56.

11. John Coplans, *Andy Warhol* (Greenwich, Conn.: New York Graphic Society, 1970), p. 8.

12. Andy Warhol, *The Philosophy of Andy Warhol: From A to B and Back Again* (New York: Harcourt Brace Jovanovich, 1975), p. 96.

13. Carter Ratcliff, *Andy Warhol* (New York: Abbeville Press, 1983), pp. 16–17.

14. Bockris, p. 69.

15. Ibid., p. 71.

16. Kornbluth, p. 18.

17. Colacello, p. 23.

18. Ibid.

19. Coplans, p. 9.

20. Jose Maria Faerna, general editor, *Warhol* (New York: Harry N. Abrams, Inc., 1997), p. 10.

Chapter 5. The Prince of Pop

1. Victor Bockris, *The Life and Death of Andy Warhol* (New York: Bantam Books, 1989), p. 94.

2. Ibid., p. 95.

3. Ibid., p. 97.

4. Richard Leslie, *Pop Art: A New Generation of Style* (New York: Todtri Productions Limited, 1997), p. 41.

5. Robert Hughes, *The Shock of the New* (New York: Alfred A. Knopf, 1981), p. 344.

6. Sister Wendy Beckett, *The Story of Painting* (New York: Dorling Kindersley Publishing, Inc., 1994), p. 380.

7. Calvin Tomkins, *Off the Wall: Robert Rauschenberg and the Art World of Our Time* (New York: Doubleday and Company, 1980), p. 36.

8. Beckett, p. 369.

9. Tomkins, p. 36.

10. Ibid., p. 184.

11. Ibid.

12. Polly Powell and Lucy Peel, *50s & 60s Style* (North Dighton, Mass.: JG Press, Inc., 1988), pp. 22–23.

13. Tomkins, p. 179.

14. Jean Stein, *Edie: An American Biography* (New York: Alfred A. Knopf, 1982), p. 195.

15. Bockris, p. 98.

16. John Coplans, *Andy Warhol* (Greenwich, Conn.: New York Graphic Society, 1970), p. 11.

17. Bockris, p. 104.

18. Hughes, p. 351.

19. Ibid., p. 348.

20. Andy Warhol and Pat Hackett, *POPism: The Warhol '60s* (New York: Harcourt Brace Jovanovich, 1980), p. 22.

21. Coplans, p. 50.

22. Bob Colacello, *Holy Terror: Andy Warhol Close Up* (New York: HarperCollins Publishers, 1990), p. 28.

23. Coplans, p. 10.

24. Beckett, p. 380.

25. Coplans, p. 11.

26. Bockris, p. 117.

27. Jose Maria Faerna, general editor, *Warhol* (New York: Harry N. Abrams, Inc., 1997), p. 14.

28. Warhol and Hackett, p. 50.

29. Bockris, p. 121.

Chapter 6. New Directions

1. Jose Maria Faerna, general editor, *Warhol* (New York: Harry N. Abrams, Inc., 1997), p. 5.

2. Andy Warhol and Pat Hackett, *POPism: The Warhol '60s* (New York: Harcourt Brace Jovanovich, 1980), p. 27.

3. Ibid., p. 61.

4. Richard Leslie, *Pop Art: A New Generation of Style* (New York: Todtri Productions Limited, 1997), p. 58.

5. Andy Warhol, *The Philosophy of Andy Warhol: From A to B and Back Again* (New York: Harcourt Brace Jovanovich, 1975), p. 144.

6. Warhol and Hackett, p. 39.

7. Victor Bockris, *The Life and Death of Andy Warhol* (New York: Bantam Books, 1989), p. 143.

8. Coplans, p. 147.

9. Bockris, p. 144.

10. Jean Stein, *Edie: An American Biography* (New York: Alfred A. Knopf, 1982), p. 200.

11. Warhol and Hackett, p. 33.

12. Ibid.

13. Bockris, p. 148.

14. John Coplans, *Andy Warhol* (Greenwich, Conn.: New York Graphic Society, 1970), p. 14.

15. Stein, p. 232.

16. Bockris, p. 158.

17. Ibid., p. 168.

18. Ibid., p. 169.

19. Stein, p. 234.

20. Warhol and Hackett, p. 132.

21. Ibid., p. 133.

22. Kurt Loder, "Andy Warhol: 1928–1987," *Rolling Stone*, April 9, 1987, p. 35.

23. Ibid.

Chapter 7. Out of Control

1. Pat Hackett, editor, *The Andy Warhol Diaries* (New York: Warner Brothers, Inc., 1989), p. 156.

2. Victor Bockris, *The Life and Death of Andy Warhol* (New York: Bantam Books, 1989), p. 192.

3. Andy Warhol and Pat Hackett, *POPism: The Warhol '60s* (New York: Harcourt Brace Jovanovich, 1980), p. 199.

4. Ibid., p. 248.

5. John Coplans, *Andy Warhol* (Greenwich, Conn.: New York Graphic Society, 1970), p. 14.

6. Bockris, p. 236.

7. Bob Colacello, *Holy Terror: Andy Warhol Close Up* (New York: HarperCollins Publishers, 1990), p. 32.

8. Bockris, p. 248.

9. Ibid., p. 238.

10. Warhol and Hackett, p. 285.

11. Andy Warhol, *The Philosophy of Andy Warhol: From A to B and Back Again* (New York: Harcourt Brace Jovanovich, 1975), p. 160.

12. Bockris, p. 250.

13. Colacello, p. 141.

14. Bockris, p. 244.

Chapter 8. The Art of Business

1. Pat Hackett, editor, *The Andy Warhol Diaries* (New York: Warner Brothers, Inc., 1989), pp. x–xi.

2. Victor Bockris, *The Life and Death of Andy Warhol* (New York: Bantam Books, 1989), p. 253.

3. Ibid., p. 254.

4. Ibid., p. 257.

5. Bob Colacello, *Holy Terror: Andy Warhol Close Up* (New York: HarperCollins Publishers, 1990), p. 58.

6. Ibid., p. 64.

7. Ibid., p. 111.

8. Ibid.

9. Ibid., p. 141.

10. Hackett, p. xiii.

11. Ibid., p. xii.

12. Colacello, p. 89.

13. Mario Amaya, *Pop Art . . . and After* (New York: The Viking Press, 1965), pp. 104–105.

14. Bockris, p. 286.

15. Andy Warhol, *The Philosophy of Andy Warhol: From A to B and Back Again* (New York: Harcourt Brace Jovanovich, 1975), p. 92.

Chapter 9. Famous Faces

1. Grace Glueck, "$15 Million Warhol Estate to Create a Foundation," *The New York Times*, February 26, 1987, p. C21.

2. Pat Hackett, editor, *The Andy Warhol Diaries* (New York: Warner Brothers, Inc., 1989), p. xv.

3. Bob Colacello, *Holy Terror: Andy Warhol Close Up* (New York: HarperCollins Publishers, 1990), p. 247.

4. Robert Hughes, "A Caterer of Repetition and Glut; Andy Warhol: 1928–1987," *Time*, March 9, 1987, p. 90.

5. Colacello, p. 265.

6. Ibid., p. 302.

7. Victor Bockris, *The Life and Death of Andy Warhol* (New York: Bantam Books, 1989), p. 293.

8. Andy Warhol, *The Philosophy of Andy Warhol: From A to B and Back Again* (New York: Harcourt Brace Jovanovich, 1975), p. 121.

9. Bokris, p. 295.

10. Colacello, p. 361.

11. Bokris, p. 298.

12. Jesse Kornbluth, *Pre-Pop Warhol* (New York: Random House, 1988), p. 9.

Chapter 10. Falling

1. Bob Colacello, *Holy Terror: Andy Warhol Close Up* (New York: HarperCollins Publishers, 1990), p. 167.

2. Victor Bockris, *The Life and Death of Andy Warhol* (New York: Bantam Books, 1989), p. 318.

3. Jose Maria Faerna, general editor, *Warhol* (New York: Harry N. Abrams, Inc., 1997), p. 48.

4. Colacello, p. 474.

5. Ibid., p. 475.

6. Bockris, p. 339.

7. Ibid., p. 340.

8. Ibid., p. 343.

9. Colacello, p. 484.

10. Richard Pearson, "Andy Warhol, Pioneer of Pop Art, Dies After Heart Attack," *Washington Post*, February 23, 1987, <http://www.washingtonpost.com/wp-srv/style/longterm/review96/fishotandywarhol.htm> (October 31, 2000).

11. D. Keith Mano, "Warhol," *National Review*, January 22, 1988, p. 502.

12. Grace Glueck, "$15 Million Warhol Estate to Create a Foundation," *The New York Times*, February 26, 1987, p. C21.

13. Ibid.

14. Mano, p. 502.

15. Kynaston McShine, editor, *Andy Warhol: A Retrospective* (New York: The Museum of Modern Art, 1989), p. 457.

Further Reading

Faerna, Jose Maria, general editor. *Warhol*. New York: Harry N. Abrams, 1997.

Hughes, Robert. "A Caterer of Repetition and Glut; Andy Warhol: 1928-1987," *Time*, March 9, 1987, pp. 90–91.

Kroll, Jack. "The Most Famous Artist," *Newsweek*, March 9, 1987, pp. 64-6.

Schaffner, Ingrid. *The Essential Andy Warhol*. New York: The Wonderland Press, 1999.

Sister Wendy Beckett. *The Story of Painting*. New York: Dorling Kindersley Publishing, Inc., 1994.

Small, Michael, Kristina Johnson, and Lee Powell. "Life Was His Canvas; Andy Warhol's Mask Protected a Special Art and Hid a Complex Personality," *People Weekly*, March 9, 1987, pp. 32-34.

Venezia, Mike. *Andy Warhol*. Danbury, Conn.: Children's Press, 1996.

Internet Addresses

The Andy Warhol Museum
<http://www.Warhol.org/>

A short biography of Warhol
<http://www.diacenter.org/permcoll/Warhol/index.html>

ArtLex Visual Arts Dictionary
<http://artlex.com/ArtLex/p/popart.html>

More Andy Warhol links
<http://www.artcyclopedia.com/artists/warhol_andy.html>

Index

Page numbers for photographs are in **boldface** type.